India

India, for those in the West, has long been – and continues
to be – the object of an almost mystical mythologising,
associated with vague notions of peace, spirituality and ascetic
superpowers. Endlessly reinvented and venerated by a Western
elite fleeing from self-styled rationalist societies, the country
continues to fascinate with its millennia of recorded history,
its pantheon of divinities whose shrines populate every street
corner, the survival of its ancient cults and rituals and its
multiplicity of languages and cultures. This time-honoured
narrative is intertwined with a new one that focuses instead
on the frenetic transformation of a society at the forefront of
digital innovation, the new spirit encapsulated in the 'India
Shining' slogan and the dynamism of its megacities that power
its phenomenal economic growth. Success stories jostle with the
daily struggles of the huge numbers of people who live without
access to potable water or a toilet in their home, and with those
engaged in a farming culture (still the largest employment
sector for the greater part of the 1.35 billion individuals who live
on the subcontinent) that is dependent on the monsoon season
and is dangerously threatened by climate change. It is the epic of
the largest democratic experiment ever attempted, which does
not know, however, how to eradicate one of the most infamous
forms of classism and racism, the caste system, exacerbated by
the Hindu nationalism of those in power today, whose laws also
discriminate against Muslims and rewrite the history books.
Nevertheless, it is difficult to find anywhere more dynamic
and optimistic on the planet – or, as Arundhati Roy writes,
'an irredeemably untidy people', able to oppose and resist for
thousands of years 'in our diverse and untidy ways'. There is a
contradictory chaos, terrible and joyous, that these pages seek
to restore, from the resistance of the Kashmiri people to that of
the country's atheists – detested by all the country's religious
communities – from the dances of the hijra in Koovagam to the
success of the wrestler Vinesh Phogat, a symbol for all women
who seek to remove themselves from the oppressive logic of
the patriarchal system. India is a tenacious country on a long
journey towards emancipation that, despite myriad difficulties
and several steps backwards, is lifting the disinherited out of
poverty.

Contents

The photographs in this issue were taken by **Gaia Squarci**, a photographer and videographer who divides her time between Milan and New York, where she teaches at the International Center of Photography. She also works with Reuters and the Italian photographic agency Prospekt. With a background in art history and photojournalism, she tends towards a personal approach far removed from the descriptive tradition of documentary photography. Her work focuses on themes linked to our connection with the natural world, disabilities and family relationships. She received POYi (Pictures of the Year International) awards for her work in 2014 and 2017 and was one of the thirty photographers under thirty chosen by Photo Boite in 2018. Her installation *Broken Screen* was selected for reGeneration3, the exhibition held at Lausanne's Musée de l'Elysée in 2015. Her photographs have appeared in titles including *The New York Times*, *Time Magazine*, *Vogue*, *The Washington Post*, the *Guardian*, *Der Spiegel*, *Internazionale*, *Io Donna* and *Corriere della Sera*.

India in Numbers

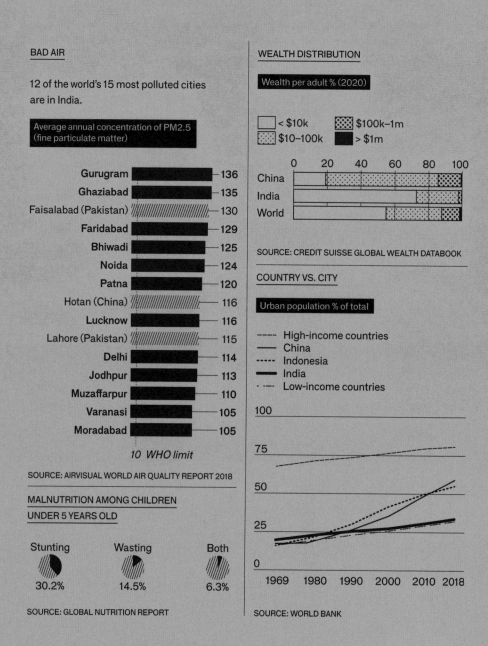

BAD AIR

12 of the world's 15 most polluted cities are in India.

Average annual concentration of PM2.5 (fine particulate matter)

Gurugram	136
Ghaziabad	135
Faisalabad (Pakistan)	130
Faridabad	129
Bhiwadi	125
Noida	124
Patna	120
Hotan (China)	116
Lucknow	116
Lahore (Pakistan)	115
Delhi	114
Jodhpur	113
Muzaffarpur	110
Varanasi	105
Moradabad	105

10 WHO limit

SOURCE: AIRVISUAL WORLD AIR QUALITY REPORT 2018

MALNUTRITION AMONG CHILDREN UNDER 5 YEARS OLD

Stunting 30.2%

Wasting 14.5%

Both 6.3%

SOURCE: GLOBAL NUTRITION REPORT

WEALTH DISTRIBUTION

Wealth per adult % (2020)

☐ < $10k   ▦ $100k–1m
▨ $10–100k   ■ > $1m

China
India
World

0 20 40 60 80 100

SOURCE: CREDIT SUISSE GLOBAL WEALTH DATABOOK

COUNTRY VS. CITY

Urban population % of total

- - - - High-income countries
——— China
· · · · · Indonesia
■■■ India
· — · — Low-income countries

100

75

50

25

0

1969 1980 1990 2000 2010 2018

SOURCE: WORLD BANK

DEATH BY SELFIE

Number of people killed while taking a selfie between March 2014 and September 2016

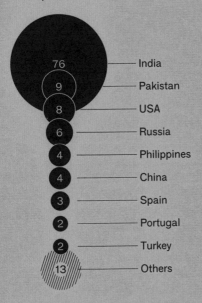

- 76 — India
- 9 — Pakistan
- 8 — USA
- 6 — Russia
- 4 — Philippines
- 4 — China
- 3 — Spain
- 2 — Portugal
- 2 — Turkey
- 13 — Others

SOURCE: CORNELL UNIVERSITY

VEGETARIANS

Rank and % by country (2019)

1

India
(38%)

2

Israel
(13%)

3

Taiwan
(12%)

4

Italy
(10%)

5

Austria/
Germany/UK
(9%)

SOURCE: WORLD ATLAS

THE WHITE STUFF

1st

India produces 176.3 million tonnes of milk per year (2018), 20% of the world's total.

SOURCE: THE ECONOMIC TIMES

ENGLISH

125

million people in India speak English, second only to the USA in terms of the number of English speakers.

SOURCE: BBC

KUMBH MELA

It is the most crowded destination in the world for religious pilgrims. On 10 February 2013, 30 million Hindu worshippers gathered near Allahabad.

Allahabad

SOURCE: NDTV

SHIP-BREAKING

The ship-breaking industry is concentrated in South Asia because of the high prices paid there for scrap metal (which is then used in local construction), low labour costs and limited regulations for safety and environmental protection.

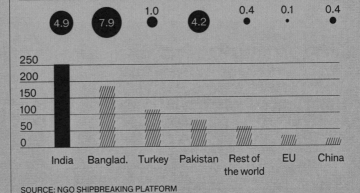

Number of ships broken and millions of tonnes of metal salvaged (2018)

	India	Banglad.	Turkey	Pakistan	Rest of the world	EU	China
Metal salvaged	4.9	7.9	1.0	4.2	0.4	0.1	0.4

SOURCE: NGO SHIPBREAKING PLATFORM

The National Sport: Cricket

Translated by Alan Thawley

India is a country of getting on for 1.4 billion people with a passion for just one sport, which explains why cricket, after football, is the world's second most followed game. As the Indian sociologist Ashis Nandy put it, cricket is 'an Indian game accidentally discovered by the British'. The Indian Premier League (IPL) was launched in 2008 and has moved the sport's centre of gravity to the Indian subcontinent, attracting the world's best cricketers, including players from England, South Africa, Australia and the West Indies. This has not always been the case, obviously. The British exported cricket to their colonies as a pastime but also as an implicit demonstration of their own civilisation: the idiosyncrasies of traditional test cricket – matches lasting up to five days, the fact that the rules are known as 'laws', the obscure terminology, the white 'flannels', the tea breaks – are the legacy of this concept of the 'gentleman's game', requiring patience and sportsmanship (not to mention free time, money and well-kept grounds), qualities that many British believed were alien to the peoples they were colonising. But the Indians saw other values in the game: its rich complexity, the infinite variations possible in each delivery and the dozen different ways for a batsman to be dismissed are, as the politician and writer Shashi Tharoor once wrote, similar to Indian classical music, in which the basic laws are just the starting point on which musicians can improvise. The game's glorious uncertainties echo ancient Indian thinking: with their sense of fatalism Indians instinctively understand that, just when think you have read the ball's trajectory and are lining it up with your bat's sweet spot, your innings can be ended by an unexpected bounce that sends the ball straight into the wicket.

The Indian game is not an elite sport. Although the first Indian cricketers were rich maharajahs and Parsees from Bombay's business community, cricket very soon became the people's sport, played in the street. In *A Corner of a Foreign Field* (Picador, 2002), the best history of cricket in India, Ramachandra Guha tells of the first true Indian champion, Palwankar Baloo, a Dalit belonging to the Chamar community of leatherworkers, being forced to sit on his own during tea breaks and drink from a clay mug while his teammates sipped from porcelain cups. But Guha argues that over time cricket has been one of the most important factors in undermining the caste system.

Since Partition cricket has often played a conciliatory role in the febrile relations between India and Pakistan, creating an intense but, on the whole, peaceful rivalry. Matches between the two nations attract fervent support: more than a billion TV viewers watched India play Pakistan in the first round of the World Cup in 2015. (Rather than following the traditional test-match format, the World Cup is a tournament of one-day cricket.) But sporting rivalry has also been a powerful diplomatic tool, used several times – for instance after the war of 1971 or during the Kashmiri insurgency of the 1990s – to reopen dialogue. It was at a cricket match in 1987 that President Zia-ul-Haq of Pakistan allegedly whispered into the ear of his Indian counterpart, Prime Minister Rajiv Gandhi, that his country had obtained the atomic bomb.

Cricket is not just about soft power, however; it has also helped to redefine Indian identity. Whereas the 1983 World Cup win at London's historic Lord's ground was unexpected, 2011's victory in the final in Mumbai was a triumph on the part of a country that had become aware of its status as a world power. The success of the IPL, modelled on English football's Premier League and the USA's NBA, has radically changed the face of cricket. By adopting the Twenty20 format, which reduces matches to around three hours in length, making them more suitable for TV viewing (complete with advertising breaks and cheerleaders), the new tournament has become a money machine, shifting the game away from its original homeland and attracting the world's most talented players to help transform the 'gentleman's game' into the first truly globalised sport.

SWISSH

Tales from Another India

VALERIO MILLEFOGLIE
Translated by Alan Thawley

On entering Vestingstraat, visitors to the Belgian city of Antwerp are greeted by the Del Rey chocolatiers and the Nicholas Diamonds jewellery store. As you continue down the street, you find yourself passing diamond shop after diamond shop after diamond shop. All the way to number 74 the shop windows on either side of the road mirror each other like a kaleidoscope that, whichever way you look at it, reflects jumbles of necklaces, rings and precious stones.

At the far end is the central railway station. And this story, too, is that of a journey, one that started out in India and arrived here in Belgium. At 52 Vestingstraat you will find the AIA, the Antwerp Indian Association, founded in 1979 by a group of diamond traders and now boasting more than five hundred members. Antwerp's diamond market, which was once the preserve of the Jewish community, is now in the hands of four hundred families of Indian origin. The first of them arrived in the late 1960s and, gradually, following in the footsteps of parents, siblings and cousins, transformed the city into an extended family business, in which marriages sealed the creation of work partnerships and other relationships. Initially they dealt in low-value uncut stones of less than a carat each, which were sent to be polished in the city of Surat in Gujarat, India's westernmost state, where the cost of skilled labour was lower. Once processed, the stones were shipped back to Antwerp to be sold in small shops. The sector remains similar to this day, but the shops have become big businesses: Antwerp accounts for 86 per cent of the global trade in rough diamonds, 90 per cent of which are sent to India and Vietnam, where wages remain low.

The majority of the Indian pioneers were Jains from the city of Palanpur. Followers of

and, most importantly, what he stood for ... At fifty-four years of age he is a young veteran very actively involved in all aspects of our organisation with a hands-on approach. I wish to be guided by him for many years to come!'

He and his fellow Indians all started out in similar ways: selling door-to-door with no car or bicycle, living two to a one-room apartment, putting in longer hours than the rest, working in the evenings or at weekends and willing to be paid less. As they explain, work always came first in these family businesses. These days they live in the residential area known as Little Bombay or Beverly Hills, with its large townhouses and tree-lined avenues leading to the nearby Den Brandt Park, complete with castle and swans circling on a little lake. Surroundings worthy of the likes of Dilip Mehta, CEO of Rosy Blue, who has been awarded the title of baron by the king of Belgium. In November 2019 Mr Mehta told *The Times of India* that, along with his children, he would be launching a new division of his company, with the aim of producing 25,000 carats of diamonds by importing synthetic roughs from China: 'Our target market will be India along with the US and Dubai.'

Meanwhile, Orra jewellers of Antwerp, with thirty-eight outlets in twenty-two cities, sells its Men of Platinum bracelet under the strapline: 'When the voice in your heart is the one you listen to. It's rare.' And on TripAdvisor one user left the following comment on the services of another jewellers, Diamond Boutique of 26 Vestingstraat: 'I bought my engagement ring here. The staff were very helpful, professional and trustworthy. Yair and his father listened to my wishes, took into account my budget and, after some negotiating, provided me with a superb diamond that sparkles wonderfully on the finger of my fiancée.'

Jainism are prohibited from hunting, fishing, dealing in arms or ivory or even cutting down trees. So the sectors in which they excel are banking and diamonds.

In a photograph on the Diamonds Creations website, Santosh Kedia, who came to Antwerp from Kolkata, sits on a black-leather chair. In one hand he holds a magnifying loupe up to his glasses; in the other he firmly grips a gemstone with a pair of tweezers. On the piece of furniture behind him you can make out the photograph of a young man on his graduation day. The job of telling his life story falls to his son, who writes that Mr Kedia 'started attending the family business under the tutelage of his grandfather and father at age seventeen. At the young age of twenty, my father was given the opportunity to move to Belgium and establish the family business in the diamond industry. It didn't take long before everyone knew my father,

India's Existential Challenge

Prime Minister Narendra Modi and the Hindu-nationalist BJP continue to pursue their right-wing fundamentalist dream of supplanting secular, multi-cultural India with a country that has room only for Hindus. Economist and writer Prem Shankar Jha argues for a rejection of this legacy of European fascism and for a reawakening of India's inclusive culture based on the concept of dharma, which allowed for centuries of religious syncretism that the nationalists now dream of sweeping away.

PREM SHANKAR JHA

Left: A guard rests in the shade at Amber Fort near Jaipur in Rajasthan, which mixes a Hindu architectural style with Islamic influences.

A quarter of a century ago, at the formal White House press conference that followed Indian Prime Minister Narasimha Rao's one-on-one meeting with President Bill Clinton during his state visit to the United States in April 1994, President Clinton heaped lavish praise upon India for doing what no other modern country had succeeded in doing before: to form a stable nation state using the tool of democracy instead of war. Clinton's point was that this was not the way in which nation states had been created in Europe in the tumultuous century that had preceded the signing of the Treaty of Westphalia in 1648.

Up until the advent of globalisation, the archetypal European nation state had hard frontiers, a unitary political structure and a culturally homogeneous population with a single national language. This uniformity had been imposed upon its citizens through a mixture of education, cultural assimilation and ethnic cleansing. The process had been violent. It had begun with the Hundred Years War (1337–1453), the most bloody and ruinous that Europe had experienced to date. This bloody phase of European history culminated in the 31-year period of the 20th century that embraced two world wars, the Russian Revolution, the Turkish pogrom against the Armenians and the Holocaust. Altogether, this 'age of catastrophe' claimed more than a hundred million lives.

But human perceptions have been slow to catch up with reality. So even after the Second World War the European nation state remained the only accepted model for a viable modern country. In the period of decolonisation that followed, 131 new nations became members of the UN. All but a few of these started out as democracies, but only two, Costa Rica and India, succeeded in sustaining and stabilising their democratic systems. The similarity, however, ends there. Costa Rica is a very small unitary state with a population of just over four million. India, by contrast, is the second largest nation in the world with a population of more than 1.35 billion, with twelve major and scores of smaller ethno-national groups, most of which have their own language, long histories as independent nations and strongly defined cultural identities.

Under the sagacious leadership of Mahatma Gandhi, the Congress Party was able to fuse them into a single nation because, unlike the majority of the other newly emergent nations, it made no attempt to create a replica of the European model. Instead, it celebrated India's diversity and used democracy and federalism to create unity within it. What emerged after three decades of fine-tuning was a 'federation of ethnicities' that the Indian Constitution explicitly describes as a 'union of states' in which each ethno-national group enjoyed an equal place within a framework defined by the constitution.

PREM SHANKAR JHA is an economist, journalist and author of over a dozen books. After his studies in Delhi and Oxford, in the 1960s he worked for the United Nations in New York and Damascus before turning to journalism and writing for the main Indian English-language newspapers – *Hindustan Times, The Times of India, Economic Times, Financial Express* and *Business Standard* – and for the weekly *Outlook* and *Tehelka*. From 1986 to 1990 he was a correspondent for *The Economist*. He also worked as a lecturer and researcher as well as media adviser to Prime Minister V.P. Singh. His most recent book is *Dawn of the Solar Age: An End to Global Warming and Fear* (Sage, 2017).

But this unique achievement is now in mortal danger. Following the 2014 general election, power passed decisively from the Congress Party into the hands of its main rival, the Bharatiya Janata Party (BJP) – the Hindu, nationalist, conservative 'party of the people' – which considers India's religious and ethnic diversity to be not its strength but its weakness and is committed to replacing it with a muscular, hyper-nationalist *Hindu Rashtra* (Hindu nation), bound together by *Hindutva* (Hindu-ness), in which non-Hindus can be accepted, albeit never on equal terms with Hindus.

In contrast to Hinduism – which is less a religion than a way of life and is at least three millennia old – both *Hindutva* and *Hindu Rashtra* were synthetic concepts adopted by those who passionately believed that the ethnic and religious diversity of India was the main stumbling block to the creation of a revolutionary movement strong enough to force the British out of the country. Vinayak Damodar Savarkar argued in his now famous book *Essentials of Hindutva* (originally published in 1923 and later retitled *Hindutva: Who Is a Hindu?*) that Hinduism had to develop the same cohesion that Muslims all over the world had shown following the fall of the Ottoman Empire and subsequent abolition of the Ottoman Caliphate, whose titular head had, for centuries, been the ruler of the Ottoman Empire. It was the rapid spread of the Khilafat movement (which sought, on the one hand, to put pressure on the Allies to restore the Caliphate and, on the other, was a Muslim pro-independence movement in India) among Indian Muslims that gave concrete shape to his concept of *Hindutva*. The Muslims, he argued, were capable of uniting rapidly to defend an institution located a quarter of a world away, one that

they barely understood, because of the unity their religion gave them. Hindus, who had no church and no clergy comparable to those of Islam and Christianity, had no such capability. If they wished to free their motherland from slavery they needed to develop something along those lines.

The three essentials of *Hindutva*, he concluded, were a common nation (*rashtra*), a common race (*jati*) and a common culture or civilisation (*sanskriti*). The influence of European fascism on his thinking was reflected in the similarity of this slogan to that of the German Nazi Party: *ein Volk, ein Reich, ein Führer* (one people, one nation, one leader). And just as the Nazis decided that Jews could not be a part of this *Volk*, Muslims and Christians could not belong to the Hindu *jati* because their *sanskriti* and their prophets originated outside the Hindu civilisation.

The threat to India arises from the fact that economic globalisation has made the European model of the nation state obsolete. Efforts by the BJP and the Hindu-nationalist Rashtriya Swayamsevak Sangh (RSS) – the parent body of the entire *Hindu Rashtra* movement – to replicate it in India has therefore come a hundred years too late. The most they can hope to achieve now is to turn India into an extreme right-wing citadel state. But, as the European experience of German fascism and the disintegration of the Soviet Union has shown, this is doomed because it can lead only to war or rebellion followed by disintegration, which would bring about the end of the great democratic experiment of building a modern nation state through democracy that Gandhi, Nehru and their colleagues in the freedom movement embarked upon in 1947.

To avert this looming disaster will be a Promethean task. It can no longer be done

> 'The guiding philosophy that has underpinned not only the modern Indian state but all major empires in India's history ... is not secularism or even pluralism but *religious syncretism.*'

by appealing to traditional caste loyalties and deal-based politics to overthrow the BJP. Since the BJP's challenge is an ideological one, it can be fought only by exposing its hollowness and inherent destructiveness and by reminding all Indians of true religious and ideological mooring, which is in religious syncretism – the constant effort to create harmony between religions and cultures in place of conflict.

The Congress Party's constant description of itself as a 'secular' party has made it an easy target for the votaries of *Hindutva* because of the aura of irreligiosity that surrounds the word. The guiding philosophy that has underpinned not only the modern Indian state but all major empires in India's history, and from which India's comfort with ethnic and religious diversity springs, is not secularism or even pluralism but *religious syncretism*. This springs from the philosophy and practice of dharma.

DHARMA – THE ANTIDOTE TO HINDUTVA

Dharma is the original faith of Vedic India. There is no reference in the Vedas, the oldest texts of the Indo-Aryan civilisation, to a Hindu dharma, because the word 'Hindu' was coined by the Persians three thousand years ago to describe the land of the Sindhu (i.e. Indus) river. It was brought to India from Persia more than two millennia later by the first Muslim invaders who came through Afghanistan and Persia.

Dharma was not a religion in the modern, exclusivist sense of the word, because the Messianic religions that are now the subject of most discourses on religion had not even been born when the word was coined. Dharma prescribed the right way to live; it dwelt at length on how people should relate to each other and to the wider world and the cosmos that surrounded them.

The *Rigveda* – a collection of Vedic hymns in Sanskrit dating from *c.* 1500–1200 BCE – differentiates between various forms of dharma, such as *prathama dharma* (the first duty), *raj dharma* (the duties of the king to his subjects) and *swadharma* (our duty to ourselves). But every one of these centres on the concept of human duty, which is 'to uphold, to support, to nourish'.

Dharma was the word Gautama Buddha used to describe his sermons on the four noble truths and the eightfold path. Western students of comparative religion have done Buddhism a disservice by suggesting it was a new religion, because this made it one among several religions, including the three Messianic religions of Judaism, Christianity and Islam. Buddha's use of the Vedic term suggests that he considered himself to be a social reformer

Right: The tomb of the Mughal Emperor Humayun in New Delhi, an example of Indo-Islamic architecture. Commissioned in 1562, it was designed by the Persian architect Mirak Mirza Ghiyath.

and not a prophet. What he had rebelled against was the corruption of dharma and the growth of *adharma*, caused by self-absorption, avarice, expensive and impoverishing ritual and Brahminical control. Buddhism was, in fact, the first great recorded rebellion against organised religion in human history. Buddha's use of the Vedic term suggests that he considered himself to be a social reformer of dharma (the Buddhist *dhamma*) and not a prophet founding a new religion.

A CRITICAL DIFFERENCE
Describing Buddhism as one of several prophetic religions, as many students of comparative religion in the West habitually do, has obscured a critical difference between Hinduism, Buddhism and other mystical religions on the one hand, and the Messianic ones – Judaism, Christianity and Islam – on the other. Messianic religions have to be professed; belonging to one requires a profession of faith and a repudiation of other faiths. It is a surrender of oneself to the 'true' God, and its reward is the possibility of gaining absolution for one's sins through repentance in *this* life.

Mystical faiths, of which dharma is the oldest, have to be lived. Only virtue in this life can gain the soul freedom from the chain of rebirth. Dharma requires no profession of faith, no submission to a single prophet – and it offers no easy absolution from sin. It is the Hindu way of referring to Buddhism as Bauddha Dharma and the remark that Hindus frequently make even today – *'Yeh mera dharma hai'* ('This is my duty') – that capture its essence.

The idea of religion as a set of beliefs that have to be practised and not merely professed is not limited to Hinduism and Buddhism but has managed to carve out a niche in Islam and Christianity as well. In the 11th and 12th centuries it found a home in a Christian sect known as the Cathars, or Albigenses, in western Europe (particularly southern France, northern Italy and Spain), and in some branches of Shia Islam such as the Alawis of Syria, Iraq and Turkey. Not surprisingly, both sects were considered heretical apostates by the clergy of orthodox Christianity and Islam. In 1209 Pope Innocent III launched a crusade against the Cathars, instructing those who joined to show no mercy and to leave it to God to sort the heretics from the true believers. As for the Alawis, the most recent of the innumerable attacks upon them is currently still under way in Syria.

But, in the sharpest possible contrast, the encounter between dharma and Islam in India has been peaceful. This first occurred in the 8th and 9th centuries when Arab traders came to Gujarat and built mosques. Not only did this not spark religious conflict but, as contemporary Jain texts recorded two centuries later, when an Afghan invader, Mahmud of Ghazni – whose empire encompassed much of present-day Afghanistan, Pakistan and north-west India – attacked the famed Somnath Temple (Temple of the Moon God) in 1025, the Arabs, who had by then been living there for generations, joined in the defence of the temple and died protecting it. The fact that Somnath was a Hindu temple did not matter to them. It had to be defended because it was important to the Hindus among whom they lived.

The second, more prolonged, interaction between the two religions took place after the establishment of the Delhi Sultanate by another Afghan invader, Muhammad Ghori, in 1192. The period that followed is the one that the RSS would like to erase from Indian memory, if not from history altogether. But it was a period in which there was an unprecedented flowering of art, music and literature. It was

Once upon a time there was a mosque. Built in 1528 in Ayodhya, in the state of Uttar Pradesh, it became the focus of an extremely long-running religious dispute – an early sign of the political manipulation and violence of Hindu extremism. According to Hindus, the Muslim emperor Babur had razed to the ground an earlier temple dedicated to the god Rama, an avatar of Vishnu born, according to tradition, on that very spot. As early as the 19th century devotees of Rama made attempts to retake the site and, following clashes with Muslims, a wall was erected to separate the two communities. The first real turning point came in 1949, when Abhiram Das, a member of a sect of militant Vaishnavites, entered the mosque in the middle of the night of 22 December and placed an idol of Rama in the building – an act of provocation that over the years has been transformed by propaganda from the Hindu Mahasabha party and the militants of the Rashtriya Swayamsevak Sangh (RSS) into the widespread belief that there was a manifestation of the god himself. A 2012 book that investigated the events, however, clearly revealed the links between Abhiram Das and the Hindu Mahasabha, which just a year earlier had plotted to kill Gandhi in an attempt to inflame conflict with Muslims. Violence erupted once more in 1992, when a crowd of 150,000 whipped up by the usual extremist groups destroyed the mosque, laying the foundations for the construction of a temple. After three decades of religious conflict, thousands of victims and a long-running legal controversy, in November 2019 the Supreme Court, on the basis of research carried out by India's national archaeological agency, declared that the site belongs to the Hindus.

the time of Amir Khusro, the first Indian poet to write in Persian. It was the time when Indian and Persian music and dance fused to create a distinct new genre, the *khayal gayaki* and the Kathak dance. It was the period during which the delicate penmanship of Persian miniature painting fused with the vivid colours of Hindu art to create a profusion of Mughal, Rajput, Kangra, Basohli and other schools of miniature painting in India. It was the time when the Indo-Islamic architecture that has given the world such wonders as the Taj Mahal and Humayun's tomb was born.

HINDUTVA'S SELECTIVE MEMORY

The ideologues of *Hindutva* ignore all this and prefer to dwell on the defeat of the Rajputs, the destruction of temples and the conversion of large numbers of Hindus to Islam during this period. This is a manufactured litany of defeat that is used to fan hyper-nationalism, Hindu religiosity and hatred towards Muslims.

But here, too, their 'memory' is selective and distorted. The Rajputs, who at the time ruled most of north India, were, admittedly, driven into the wilds of Rajasthan, but their defeat came about through the superior military technology of the invaders – of cavalry over elephants and of archers over infantry – and not from anything innately superior about the Muslim warriors. On the contrary, the conquerors recognised the valour of the Rajputs and quickly inducted them into their armies.

The votaries of *Hindutva* harp on endlessly about the damage the Muslim invaders did to Hindu polity and society, but again they choose to ignore the fact that the same Muslim dynasties saved India from the greatest scourge of the Middle Ages: the Mongol invasions that ravaged Europe. Like other impoverished groups from the Asian steppes, the Mongols first tried to invade India. Their initial foray in 1241 took the Delhi Sultanate by surprise, and the Mongols were able to reach as far as Lahore, now Pakistan's most beautiful city, and sack it at their leisure. But that was the last time they were able to enter the plains of India. Ghiyasuddin Balban, the ruler in Delhi at the time, created a standing army – India's first – built a string of forts along the border and prevented all subsequent invaders from getting far into the plains of Hindustan. After his death in 1287, another warrior king of the Delhi Sultanate, Alauddin Khilji, inflicted two successive defeats on the Mongols in 1304 and 1305 that were so decisive that they turned their attention towards Europe and never returned.

Admittedly, temples were destroyed and precious art, sculpture and architecture irretrievably lost, but the motive of the invaders, like that of invaders throughout history, was pillage not forced conversion to Islam. All but a fraction of the conversions that took place over the following four hundred years were voluntary. The converts came from the lower Hindu castes, and they converted because Islam offered an escape from the iniquities of caste – in much the same way as Buddhism had done two thousand years earlier, and as the *bhakti* (devotion) anti-Brahmin movement in south India had been doing since the 7th century, well before the arrival of the Muslims. Far from being a blot on the conquerors, these conversions were an impeachment of the Brahminical, temple-centred Hinduism from which they had been systematically excluded.

RECONCILIATION BETWEEN HINDUISM AND ISLAM

In northern India the encounter between Islam and Hinduism proved beneficial to both in important ways that the Sangh

Right: The Gyanvapi Mosque (1669) in the city centre of Varanasi. The area has been heavily militarised since 2018 when Narendra Modi first ordered excavations that uncovered the remains of a pre-existing Hindu temple, creating a corridor that connects the remains of the temple to the banks of the Ganges.

THE GUJARAT POGROM

On 27 February 2002 a train filled with Hindu pilgrims returning from Ayodhya was attacked by a crowd of around two thousand people near Godhra railway station. A fire broke out on the train in which fifty-nine people lost their lives. The subsequent trials and parliamentary commissions have left many doubts as to whether it was an Islamic terrorist attack (the official version), was instigated by a different group or was an accident. News of the attack on the pilgrims sparked a genuine anti-Muslim pogrom across the state of Gujarat: around two thousand people were massacred by a murderous crowd, 150,000 were forced

to leave their homes and hundreds of mosques and Islamic places of worship were destroyed. The impression was that Gujarat's state government – led by a certain Narendra Modi, then newly elected chief minister – had at best stood by and let the mob do its work. The greatest extent of compassion expressed by India's future prime minister was contained in his cryptic remark that 'if we are driving a car, we are a driver, and someone else is driving a car and we're sitting behind, even then if a puppy comes under the wheel, will it be painful or not? Of course it is.' After months of unrest, in March 2003 Islamic terrorists took revenge: thirteen attacks rocked Mumbai, targeting a number of symbolic locations, including the Stock Exchange, and killing 257 people. Sadly, the Gujarat pogrom was neither the first nor the last in India. In 1984 the violence that broke out after the assassination of Prime Minister Indira Gandhi was followed by the massacre of three thousand Sikhs in Delhi, while recent events have included severe clashes in Muzaffarnagar, Uttar Pradesh, which claimed the lives of forty-three Muslims and twenty Hindus in 2013, and the 2020 Delhi riots – chiefly Hindu mobs attacking Muslims – that left fifty-three dead.

Parivar (an umbrella term for the 'family' – *parivar* in Hindi – of right-wing Hindu-nationalist organisations) prefers not to remember. In Hinduism it weakened the link between religion and the state by cutting off the single most important source of patronage to the temples. As state patronage dwindled, Brahmins, who had previously flocked to the temples, were forced to remain in their villages and tend to the spiritual needs of the villagers. The emphasis in their functions, therefore, shifted from presiding over elaborate temple rites to providing guidance on the issues the villagers faced in their every-day lives. The importance of ritual in Hinduism therefore declined and that of dharma increased.

Hinduism met the challenge from Sufi Islam by disseminating the core ideas of dharma, already espoused and rejuvenated by the *bhakti* movement, through the literature, poetry and song of Tulsidas, Surdas, Kabir, Rahim, Mira Bai, Tukaram, Chokhamela and a host of lesser-known poets, bards and singers. The interaction between the two made Hinduism access-ible and mellowed Islam further, to the point where, except for scripture, little remained of what had divided the one from the other. No couplet I know captures this more succinctly than one by the late-15th-century poet Kabir that I learned as a child and have never forgotten:

> *Moko kahaan dhoondhate bande, Mai to tere paas me;*
> *Na Mai Mandir, na Mai Masjid, naa Kaaba Kailash me.*

(Where dost thou seek me, oh devotee, for I am right beside thee;
Not in a temple, nor in a mosque, not at the Qaaba, nor on Mount Kailash, shalt thou find me.)

This profound reconciliation between Hinduism and Sufi Islam is perhaps best reflected in the writings of Guru Nanak and the other *gurus* of Sikhism. And it was not confined to the villages. It was codified by no less august a person than Emperor Akbar the Great in the 16th century as the *Din-e Ilahi,* the religion of God, at the height of the Mughal Empire. Some British historians have hailed it as an attempt at founding a new faith based on universal tolerance; others have dismissed it as a religion that never had more than nine-teen followers. In fact, Akbar had no such intention. The *Din-e Ilahi* was no more than a distillation of what today's corpo-rate world would call 'current best prac-tices' of the heterodox population of India. It propagated *sulh-i-kul* – universal peace – and urged ten virtues upon the realm. Among these were: being open minded and well meaning; refraining from hostile actions; countering anger with restraint; abstinence from worldly desires; frequent meditation on the consequences of one's actions and 'good society with brothers so that *their will may have precedence over one's own*' – in short, putting the well-being of one's fellows ahead of one's own. Akbar's goal was not to proselytise. Unlike the Buddhist edicts of the great Mauryan emperor, Ashoka, 1,800 years earlier, Akbar issued no commands and nor did he create a religious police to oversee their observance.

The significance of the *Din-e Ilahi* lies in *what it did not prescribe*: it did *not* ascribe primacy to Islam, and it did *not* give a special place to Muslim clergy within the structure of the state. Instead, it declared emphatically that 'he [the emperor, i.e. the state] would recognise no difference between religions, his object being to unite all men in a common bond of peace'. The entire document was, therefore, a restatement of dharma in a contemporary form. If any 'religion' can claim to have emerged the victor in the grand ideological battle that ensued after the arrival of Islam in India, it is dharma.

Among Hindus, the practice of dharma has been – and remains – sullied by its endorsement of the notion of ritual purity and pollution that is associated with caste. But its core idea, that true religion is not what we preach but what we practise, has remained the driving force behind all movements for religious reform from the Buddha to the present day. It was with this that the monk Swami Vivekananda electrified the Parliament of the World's Religions in Chicago in 1893, by explaining that Hinduism does not merely tolerate but accepts all the great religions of the world because they are like different paths up the same mountain or different rivers that flow into the same sea.

Even the blood-soaked partition of India and Pakistan in 1947 did not kill off the syncretic impulse in Islam. It has led to a sustained study in Pakistan of the writings of Dara Shikoh, the grandson of Akbar, and his successor Shah Jahan's eldest son and heir apparent. Dara Shikoh was a scholar of Sanskrit and translator of the *Bhagavad Gita*, one of Hinduism's holiest texts. He had made no secret of his fascination with *Din-e Ilahi* and of his intention to propagate it throughout his realm before his life was cut short in 1659 by his more religiously orthodox youngest brother Aurangzeb.

In 2010 the noted Pakistani playwright Shahid Nadeem wrote a play, *Dara*, that highlighted his syncretism as a protest against the rampant Islamic sectarianism that Partition had unleashed upon Pakistan and was, even then, tearing it apart. Three years later two Pakistani historians from Government College University Faisalabad published a peer-reviewed paper in the *International Journal of History and Research* entitled 'Dara Shikoh: Mystical and Philosophical Discourse', which highlighted his belief that 'the mystical traditions of both Hinduism and Islam spoke of the same truth'.

This is the awe-inspiring syncretism of religion in the land of dharma. It is what has made Indian Muslims virtually immune to the lure of the Islamic State in Syria and Iraq: of the *c.* 30,000 foreign fighters who joined the organisation, the number of Indian Muslims was only 106 – and, of these, only three went directly from India; the rest were recruited while they were migrant workers in the Gulf.

This is the awe-inspiring syncretism of India that the votaries of *Hindutva* and *Hindu Rashtra* are bent upon destroying. *Hindutva* is therefore the complete antithesis of dharma.

NARENDRA MODI

Born in 1950 to a humble family in Gujarat,
Modi grew up selling tea on the streets and
frequenting the local branch of the RSS, the
launch pad for his rise in the BJP. After years
of activism he won the elections in Gujarat,
accusing the outgoing chief minister of
corruption. Coming to power a few months
after the 9/11 attacks in New York, he stoked
the fires of anti-Muslim sentiment, and his
career has been tarnished by suspicions of his
involvement in the 2002 pogroms. Over the
course of three successive terms in Gujarat, he
combined nationalist rhetoric with the image
of a free-market reformer, winning the support
of leading industrialists whose backing was a
decisive factor in his 2014 general election win.
During his first term in office he surprised
many with a demonetisation programme:
citizens were given just one and a half
months to get rid of their 1,000- and
500-rupee banknotes (86 per cent of the
cash in circulation), which were declared
out of circulation from 30 December 2016.
After weeks of chaos and disruption –
including endless queues at banks suffering
cash shortages – the situation stabilised.
However, the economy does not appear to
have benefited from the measure, nor from
the attempt in 2017 to combat tax evasion
– a historic tax reform that decreased fiscal
pressure with the introduction of a single
consumption tax – and unemployment actually
grew throughout Modi's first term in office,
from 2.2 per cent in 2012 to 6.1 per cent in
2018. This did not prevent him from gaining an
absolute majority to win a second term in 2019.

THE ORIGINS OF HINDUTVA

In the 1920s the desire to militarise Hinduism could perhaps have been condoned, for it was a counsel of despair. The Congress was still only a middle-class debating society, Mahatma Gandhi's doctrine of *satyagraha* (passive resistance to paralyse government) was still largely untried and the British had taken to shooting or hanging freedom fighters after labelling them as terrorists. But the last shred of justification for this was lost when India gained its freedom, for the creation of Pakistan had fulfilled at least one of the goals of the RSS – it had rid India of all the Muslims who did not accept that they were part of Savarkar's Hindu *sanskriti*.

The third who remained in India had therefore pledged their allegiance to the country by staying. So what fuelled the frantic rage against Partition that the RSS vented in the immediate aftermath of independence? Why did they rejoice openly when Mahatma Gandhi was assassinated and lionise his assassin Nathuram Godse? And what has made them continue to demonise Indian Muslims after they had ceased to be a threat to 'Hindu' India? The explanation is that the RSS's goal was not simply to oust the British from India but to take their place in order to create a Hindu India moulded to fit their image of *Hindu Rashtra*.

Today the Sangh Parivar is trying to pass Savarkar and Keshav Baliram Hedgewar, the founder of the RSS, off as freedom fighters. But C.P. Bhishikar, who wrote a biography of Hedgewar – along with some remarks made by Hedgewar's successor Madhav Sadashiv Golwalkar – showed that from the Dandi Salt March in 1929 up to Gandhi's Quit India call in 1940, the RSS stoutly opposed every attempt to secure freedom through the Gandhian way of *satyagraha* and even offered its cohorts to the government to act as civil guards to quell the unrest that Gandhi's call would generate. To the RSS, freedom was less important than power. It needed more time to create the *Hindutva* legions with which it hoped to wrest control. And, as with fascism in Europe, it required an enemy that it could persuade people to hate and fear in order to justify their creation.

Caught out by Partition – which Mountbatten announced only in March 1947 – the RSS made an attempt, nonetheless, to seize power in the wake of the turmoil unleashed by Partition and the assassination of Mahatma Gandhi. Consequently it was banned for several years, but the seizure of power remained its unswerving goal through all its subsequent vicissitudes.

WHAT NOW?

The BJP's second victory in 2019 has removed all the political and constitutional hurdles to achieving the goal that the RSS set itself in 1923. Narendra Modi has brought it to power on a wave that will almost certainly sweep over time through the state-assembly elections as well and give it the majority in the upper house of parliament that it needs to change the Indian Constitution. But Modi and the RSS are in a hurry and have little appetite for the debates that will rage in parliament and civil society when the government presents bills for radically altering the constitution.

As a result it is resorting to legal trickery to start a process of ethnic cleansing and to dissolve the constitutional safeguards that protect India's 'federation of ethnicities'.

This began in earnest within weeks of the BJP being returned to power. The government finalised a national register of citizens in Assam that left out 1.9 million people, some of whom had lived in the state with their families and children for five or more decades. To house them 'temporarily' until they are repatriated to Bangladesh or elsewhere, the government is building 'detention' camps for them all over Assam and has issued a directive to the administrative heads of all of India's 724 districts to earmark sites for building similar camps in their districts when the need for them arises. That the intended targets are Muslim immigrants from Bangladesh became apparent when the BJP government in Assam asked for an amendment to the citizenship rules that would allow it to limit repatriation to them alone. This amendment, called the Citizenship Amendment Act, became necessary when it was realised that a large proportion of those identified as illegal immigrants were Hindus who had been driven out by the Pakistani Army in 1971 or by hostile villagers who had occupied their land and did not allow them to return to their villages after the war ended.

The assault on India's religious syncretism has been launched in the one place where it had continued to flourish until well after Partition and where it still survives today. This is the state of Jammu and Kashmir. On 5 August 2019 the government used a constitutional sleight of hand to dissolve the statehood of Kashmir and turn it into a union territory to be administered directly from Delhi without any reference to its legislature or people.

The closest parallel in history to the BJP's victory this year is Hitler's return to power in March 1933. The Nazi campaign, too, was based upon hatred and paranoia. Its targets were principally the Jews but also the gypsies – whom they considered another inferior, polluting race – and the communists. Like the BJP today, the Nazis took advantage of the collapse of the German economy after the Wall Street Crash of 1929 to seize power in 1930 with 18 per cent of the vote. Three years later their hate rhetoric had pushed up their vote to 43 per cent. Within days of the January 1933 results its storm-troopers duped a communist sympathiser into setting the German parliament building on fire and helped him do it. In the anti-communist hysteria that followed Hitler was able to win the March 1933 elections, persuade President Hindenburg and the German parliament to pass an enabling act giving him extraordinary powers, declare him chancellor for life and thus destroy the Weimar Republic. His storm-troopers then systematically attacked Jews, gypsies and communists, set up internment camps and later initiated the programme of mass extermination in the gas chambers.

The Nazi experiment ended in the defeat, destruction and dissection of pre-war Germany. The *Hindutva* experiment has just begun, and we cannot predict with certainty where it will end, but the future looks grim. The Modi government is due to remain in power until May 2024. Only an opposition in parliament and civil society that rediscovers dharma and pits it against *Hindutva* has any chance of stopping the headlong rush to disaster. ✒

IN/VISIBLE:
A Woman's Place in India

TISHANI DOSHI

Given the extraordinary growth of the Indian economy
in recent years, why are the numbers of women in the
workplace in India falling? Small advances in legislation
and the outcry provoked by a number of high-profile
acts of violence against women have not proved resilient
enough to make a dent in a patriarchal model of society
that seeks to confine women to domestic duties.

A woman on the street in Neemli, Rajasthan.

29

I

In April 2006 I visited the village of Koovagam in Tamil Nadu to cover India's largest transgender gathering. For months before the festival I had been interviewing a group of transgender people, who in India are known by a variety of names – hijras, aravanis, kothis – and they had consented to my cameraman and I travelling with them.

The festival itself takes place over one fevered night in a one-street village, but for days leading up to it we stayed in the nearby town of Viluppuram, where transgender communities conducted beauty contests and HIV-awareness campaigns. The hotel we were all staying at was alive with action. Hijras spilled out of rooms, leaning against bannisters, framing themselves picturesquely in doorways. All manner of men walked up and down the stairs and in and out of rooms looking for sex. The mother of our group was matter of fact about this. Prostitution paid the bills. It would take another eight years (April 2014) for the Supreme Court to grant hijras their status as third gender, allowing them to hold ration cards and other government documents that would allow them to participate in civic life. But in 2006 they were still largely disenfranchised, relying primarily upon begging and prostitution to make a living.

Among the many transactionary encounters of sex that my cameraman and I witnessed over those days, there was space for tenderness as well. We sat in bedrooms and listened to love stories between cis and trans, rich and poor, stories of Bollywoodian and Shakespearean power. We spent afternoons gathered around a bed, looking at the baubles of paramours spread out for us to coo over: tokens to prove they were women who were loved and desired by men.

On the final evening of the festival we travelled to the village of Koovagam together, our entire band dressed in bridal finery. Everyone drifted off under the street lamps in different directions. The whole scene was a mixture of carnival and pilgrimage. Thousands of people thrown into one heaving mass. There were fairground rides, candyfloss and peanut stands, music blared from all corners. Everything and everyone was a hologram. Look one way, you'd see a man, look another, you'd see a woman. It made me think of the famous lines from the *bhakti* poet Dasimayya, who in the 10th century wrote:

TISHANI DOSHI is an award-winning poet, novelist and dancer. Her most recent books are *Girls Are Coming Out of the Woods* (Bloodaxe USA, UK/HarperCollins India, 2017), shortlisted for the Ted Hughes Poetry Award, and a novel, *Small Days and Nights* (Norton USA/Bloomsbury UK, India, 2020), shortlisted for the RSL Ondaatje Prize and a New York Times Bestsellers Editor's Choice. *A God at the Door* (poems) was published in spring 2021 by Copper Canyon (USA), Bloodaxe (UK) and HarperCollins (India). She is a visiting professor of creative writing at NYU, Abu Dhabi, and otherwise lives on a beach in Tamil Nadu, India.

'Heterosexuals paid for sex with hijras because it was cheaper – you didn't have to rent a hotel room or buy her food or a beer, you could just take her behind a truck.'

If they see
breasts and long hair coming
they call it woman,
if beard and whiskers
they call it man:
but, look, the self that hovers
in between
is neither man nor woman
O Ramanatha.

The temple, which was the central fixture of the event, conducted mass marriage ceremonies all night. Hijras offered themselves as brides to Aravan. The legend of the warrior-prince Aravan, a character from the *Mahabharata*, is that he was a man of perfect qualities but was destined to die young in battle. Aravan was willing to lay down his life on the condition that he could know marital bliss beforehand (i.e. lose his virginity). The only woman who would agree to becoming a widow was a hijra. And so, we watched the re-enactment of this myth again and again. Brides kept streaming into the temple. Some married flesh-and-blood Aravans, but for most, their god-husband was symbolic.

That night my cameraman and I slept on the roof of the temple while the small south Indian village glittered all around us. Couples paired off to have sex in the surrounding sugarcane fields, enjoying the bliss of their wedding night. The more spiritually minded hijras retired to their hotel rooms. In the morning the grieving began. Hijras went through the rituals of widowhood – breaking their bangles, beating their chests and wailing, bathing

in the temple water tank and then draping themselves in white widows' saris before making their way home. Next year they would do this all over again.

I remember thinking then, as I still do, that what would be called a gay parade in another part of the world was something much more complicated in India. Yes, it was a visual display of celebrating queer identity, but here it combined the carnival, carnal and spiritual, and it was all happening in a one-street village not a pulsing urban centre. Here, the myths were so kaleidoscopic so as to allow all kinds of gender fluidity. And even though transgender people normally inhabited the fringes of society in India, there were still occasions where they could occupy a central space.

Later I would think about how I'd never been witness to such a range of male desire: software engineers who came to the festival to cross-dress and prance around, who were gay but who could never tell their parents they were gay; hijras who were trapped in their bodies, who had run away from towns and cities all over the country, who had formed new households, new communities – some who had castrated themselves, others who were saving for a full sex change and hormonal treatment, still others who wore saris but had stubble on their chins and seemed content to float in this gender ambiguity; auto drivers and bank tellers who were heterosexual but who paid for sex with hijras because it was cheaper – you didn't have to rent a hotel room or buy her food or a beer, you could just take her behind a truck.

The entire spectrum of Indian masculinity leaked over any binary ideas I'd had of gender and sexuality. And while there was something exhilarating about a small town in south India being the playground for such challenging of gender stereotypes, I understood that it moved in one direction only. This was a display of male longing for the feminine, to be able to access feminine power and dissolve in it. And I thought: where is the space for women in India who feel similarly trapped in their bodies? Is it possible to imagine a visible space for women in India to access male power?

II

On 16 December 2012 a 23-year-old woman called Jyoti Singh was returning home from the cinema with a friend, Awindra Pandey, after watching an evening show of *Life of Pi*. She worked nights in an IBM call centre and was putting herself through medical college. That evening she and Awindra climbed on to a white bus to catch a ride home. There were five other passengers on the bus, all young men. For an hour they gang-raped Jyoti, bit her entire body with their teeth, used an iron bar to tear out most of her intestines. The driver went first, the other men followed. Whenever Awindra tried to help, he was beaten with the iron rod. After the men were finished, they threw the half-naked bodies of Awindra and Jyoti out of the moving bus, on the side of the road, where they were eventually found by the police.

Jyoti Singh succumbed to her injuries twelve days later, but not before giving an account of what happened, the names of her perpetrators and the acts they committed on her body. She wrote on a piece of paper for the doctors: 'I want to survive.'

The world knows some or most of these details now. We know the horrific story of Jyoti Singh because, even though a rape is reported every fifteen minutes in India, this is the story that catalysed us as a nation and rippled out into the world.

In September 1992 there had been a similarly catalysing event. Bhanwari Devi, a Dalit social worker in Rajasthan, was attacked in the fields she was working in with her husband by five high-caste men. Two of them beat her husband with sticks, holding him down, while the other three took turns raping her. The men were angry because Bhanwari Devi had been trying to prevent a child marriage from happening in one of the men's families. A child bride herself, Devi worked with a grassroots organisation, going from door to door, talking to women about the benefits of family planning and discouraging them from dowry marriages and female foeticide and infanticide.

Devi filed her rape complaint in the police station but was asked to leave her skirt as 'evidence' and so had to use her husband's blood-stained turban to cover herself and walk three kilometres to the village at 1 a.m. She was accused of lying and was ostracised by villagers. The judge cleared her accused rapists of all charges because he believed (among other reasons) that men of different castes could not participate in a gang-rape, older men of sixty or seventy cannot rape, a village head cannot rape, a member of a high caste cannot rape a lower-caste woman. And so on. The judgement brought protestors out into the streets, but despite several interventions by activists and the National Commission for Women, Devi did not get justice. Her case did, however, lead the way in 1997 to setting up the most important laws in India to protect women in the workplace from sexual harassment, the Vishaka Guidelines.

There have been catalysing events before and after Bhanwari Devi and Jyoti

Above: A hijra at a birthday party. Hijras – transgender, transsexual or intersex individuals pushed to the margins of society – are often invited to ceremonies because their blessings are considered good luck.

Above: The hands of Gouri Sharma, who is transgender, at Delhi Queer Pride.

THE PASSENGER Tishani Doshi

Singh. Every year, every month, every day if you look in the newspapers, there is an act of violence against a girl or woman in India that is so terrible, so incredible, it makes you believe that this event will overhaul society. The problem with Indian society is that there are several layers of entrenchment at work. Patriarchy is the shroud that suffocates the entire nation, but the underlying threads of caste and religion are equally stifling. Change, therefore, can never be completely transformative, it must always be incremental. And there can be no conviction that once certain rights are secured there will be no chance of falling back.

III

As a child growing up in Madras, my family would meet for lunch every Sunday at my paternal grandfather's house. My grandfather wasn't a chatty man, but every Sunday he would ask in Gujarati, by way of greeting, 'Tishani, have you learned to make rotis yet?' And every Sunday I'd shake my head and run off.

In that house, the dining table was small, so we ate in turns. Men first, children second, women last. Because we had more women in our family, and because I was a tomboy and always hungry, I got to eat with the men. In an unarticulated feminist move, I had understood the kitchen as a place of entrapment. I had no wish to enter there. I sat with my grandfather, father, brother and uncles, helping myself to fresh, hot food, while my cousins (all girls) and aunts brought fresh rotis and pappads from the kitchen. After eating their fill the men would slip off to sleep on couches for an afternoon nap, and I would do the same.

Ours was a traditional family structure. Women stayed at home. Men were breadwinners who worked six days of the

HIJRAS

Venerated and admired in ancient India, now discriminated against and marginalised, hijras are transgender individuals who live on the margins of society in communities welcoming to those who undergo surgery or hormone treatments to change sex or who exhibit ambiguous genital configurations. The term hijra identifies a community that is aware of the role it plays in the traditional Indian religious landscape and embraces this choice. Their history dates back to the 4th century BCE: as fertility priests they were sacred, semi-divine figures; under the Mughal Empire they were chosen as advisors, confidants and guardians of the royal palace. After British colonisation their role changed radically: today hijras – numbering around three million – live in communities in the shanty towns of India's big cities, thrown out by their families and subject to threats and brutal violence. Wrapped in colourful saris and swathed in jingling jewellery, they usually meet in extremely crowded houses, where the *nayak*, their spiritual guide, is surrounded by followers known as *chelas*. Hijras must respect the community's hierarchy and follow certain rules. There are only three occupations open to them: *badhai*, singing and dancing at weddings or other ceremonies; *mangti*, begging; and *dhanda*, prostitution, which is the main cause of the prevalence of HIV among them. In spite of the official recognition of the third sex in 2014, hijras have yet to find a place in Indian society.

week in the family business. Sunday was the one day they could take an afternoon nap. My father and uncles all still work six days a week, even though they are long past retirement age. All my girl cousins, with the exception of two, work either full or part time and know how to make rotis. I still have not learned how to make rotis, but I do work.

IV

In 2018 there was a street-art graffiti poster that went viral. It showed a young girl rolling rotis, looking up beseechingly. The text in Hindi beside her said: *How will you eat the rotis made by her hand, when you won't even allow your daughters to be born?* It was part of Prime Minister Narendra Modi's *Beti Bachao, Beti Padhao* (Save the Girl Child, Educate the Girl Child) campaign, and it came to represent every contradiction inherent in the treatment of women and girls in India.

SOME STATISTICS FIRST:
· In 2019 for every 1,000 boys born in India there were only 930 females.
· Indian women contribute to only one-sixth of the economic output (one of the lowest shares in the world – half the global average).
· Despite increases in female literacy and decrease in fertility rates the proportion of women in the workplace in India dropped from 35 per cent in 2015 to 26 per cent in 2018.
· Among the G20 countries, only women in Saudi Arabia are less likely to work than Indian women.
· 49 per cent of women between fifteen and twenty-four are not involved in education or employment training compared with 8.1 per cent of males.
· Women are paid 62 per cent of what men earn for the same job.

· Were India to rebalance its workforce, the IMF estimates that the country would be 27 per cent richer.
· Two-thirds of the population in India lives in the countryside, and agriculture accounts for over half of all female employment.
· Less than 13 per cent of agricultural land is controlled by women.
· 41 per cent of young Indians believe it is better if married women do not work.
· The rate of suicide among Indian women is higher than among men, with more than twenty thousand housewives committing suicide each year.
· Indian women do 90 per cent of the housework, which is the highest proportion in the world.
· Only one in eight members of parliament is a woman in India; only two out of twenty-three Supreme Court judges are female.

People have come to expect contradictions in India. The Hindu deities of wealth and learning are goddesses – Lakshmi and Saraswati – and yet women in the house aren't always honoured as goddesses. Female literacy and urbanisation are on the rise and fertility rates have dropped, and while in any other developing country this would indicate that women have more time for their careers, in India the employment rates of women have sharply reduced. What is happening?

A visitor to India might believe the story that India is telling itself – that women form a central place in the economy. Because everywhere you look you see women working, unlike groups of men that you frequently see loitering in every Indian town. This is rare with women. Women always seem to be doing something – walking with shopping bags, firewood, pots of water, herding goats, cows, children. Even

'The problem with Indian society is that there are several layers of entrenchment at work. Patriarchy is the shroud that suffocates the entire nation, but the underlying threads of caste and religion are equally stifling.'

if we disregard the gigantic amount of daily invisible domestic labour that women contribute, which is not counted as part of the GDP, the numbers still point in a worrying direction. Why is it that with girls doing so much better than boys at school, employment figures don't reflect this?

There are infrastructural issues, of course: things might be better if the government could create better childcare benefits, maternity-leave packages, safer commutes, better-lit streets. But the single determining factor is the patriarchal social expectation that women are expected to do all the work at home. They must cook, clean, look after the young and the elderly. If they want to work, their families would happily pocket the extra income, but essentially there would be no time for sleep or leisure. This has manifested in something called 'the marriage penalty'. Statistics show that while there is a rise in the workforce of unmarried women, the numbers of married women in the workforce have remained static in urban areas and declined in rural areas, because to do all the work at home and to have a job is too hard.

As one journalist put it, 'Women find it easier to drop out than drop dead from overwork.'

v

In 2018 the Thomas Reuters Foundation stated that India was the most dangerous country in the world for a woman to live. They were taking into account statistics for sexual violence, human trafficking, acid attacks, female foeticide and infanticide, honour killings, forced marriages, etc. The data showed that crimes against women in India had risen by 83 per cent between 2007 and 2016, with four cases of rape reported every hour.

The way violence on this scale works is this: one day the circle will touch you. It cannot remain an abstraction. Even if it doesn't touch you directly, it will touch someone close to you.

On 5 October 2016 a photographer and perfumer, Monika Ghurde, was killed in her apartment in Goa. Monika and I had been neighbours and friends in Madras for many years before she relocated to Goa. She had recently separated from her husband and was living alone in an affluent apartment complex. Her body was found tied to the bed, half naked and with signs of strangulation. Soon after it was determined that the perpetrator of the crime was the 21-year-old security guard in the same building.

In the aftermath of her death, newspapers dwelled on the lurid aspects of the crime. She was a young, attractive woman, and there was endless speculation about her life, her character, her privilege, her marital status in many of the articles about her death. For friends who knew her it seemed unbearable that she had been killed in such a fashion, that she would forever be remembered as this dead girl tied to her bed, that a woman dies horribly and must die again and again in the retelling. In an effort to counter the established narrative of physical

THE PASSENGER   Tishani Doshi

and sexual violence against women that dehumanises victims, five friends and I decided to write tributes to Monika and publish them in different media so that the measure of her life wouldn't necessarily be commensurate with the nature of her death. The idea was to remember that each woman who has been killed is a person not a statistic.

Three years after her murder things are still unclear. The guard is being submitted for various psychological treatments, and conspiracy theories abound. There is a sense that we will never know what really happened, but the fact is she is dead. If you google her name, a frequent search request is: *Monika Ghurde dead body pics.*

The way violence on this scale works is that it makes women in India fear to undertake the simple act of living alone. Monika herself had been nervous about living on her own; she took martial-arts lessons and was cautious to the point of being paranoid about her safety. Politicians say things like, if you want to keep your daughters safe you must park them at home like cars so they won't get scratched, even though all evidence points to the home as being one of the most dangerous places for women. Monika was at home. Monika was killed.

The way violence on this scale works is that in a country such as India, a population of women the size of Sri Lanka

can be disappeared. Not just literally but metaphorically as well. In a BBC story it was revealed that twenty-one million Indian women had been denied the right to vote in the 2019 elections because their names were not found on the electoral register. It was as if they simply did not exist. There was another story in which it was revealed that there are villages in India's sugarcane belt where there are women with missing wombs because they are forced to have hysterectomies so as to not miss days of work due to menstrual cycles.

If you lay these stories one against the other, one on top of the other, what you get is a transient chimera of the story of women in India. On one hand, a country that attributes all creation to the female principle, that worships goddesses with fervour in all forms, that prays dutifully at roadside mother shrines, that venerates the idea of mother, of procreation as sacrosanct; on the other hand, the story in homes and in the streets, in corporations and universities, in the church, the temple and the mosque – a story of unremitting violence against women that continues and continues.

VI

It is important to end with resilience, to remember that a history of feminist resistance runs deep in India.

Women were an integral part of India's freedom movement from the British, leading the struggle when many of the men were locked up in prison. In the 1970s there was the eco-feminist Chipko movement in the Himalayas, a grassroots organisation led mostly by women who, to prevent the logging of trees in their forests, strapped themselves around tree trunks.

One of the most brave and daring acts of recent protest was in 2004, when twelve

'The BJP government wants to move forward with the feeling of a world economic superpower, while half of the population still has no access to toilets.'

middle-aged Manipuri women stripped naked outside the headquarters of the Assam Rifles in Imphal with a sign across their chests that read: Indian Army Rape Us. The night before, a young woman, Thangjam Manorama Devi, had been picked up from her house on the pretext of being a militant by the army in a 'night operation'. Hours later she was found dead on the road. She had been raped and there were sixteen bullet wounds to her genitals. For years the Mothers of Manipur (Meira Paibi or women torchbearers), a women's civil rights group, had been protesting to repeal the controversial AFSPA, the Armed Forces Special Powers Act, which gives the Indian Army immunity in 'disturbed' parts of the country such as the north-east and Kashmir and has led to a large-scale brutalisation of the population, especially women.

With the rape and murder of Manorama, these women could not just hold a candle-light vigil. Something had changed. They had to use their bodies as a tool. They thought, if it is so easy to be raped, then why not walk naked? They did not even tell their husbands of their plans. They stood outside naked, some of them over sixty years old, and chanted, 'Rape us, kill us! Rape us, kill us. We are all Manorama's mothers. Come, rape us, you bastards!'

The protest caused huge outrage, and the twelve women were arrested and jailed for three months. The Assam Rifles soon moved out of the area, and Manorama's family were given financial compensation, but none of her killers has been apprehended.

Another woman who has single-handedly been trying to repeal AFSPA is Irom Sharmila, also a Manipuri woman, known as the 'Iron Lady', who fasted for sixteen years as a protest. She said she would not eat, drink, comb her hair, look in a mirror or meet her mother until this draconian law was changed. Irom was arrested on a charge of attempting to commit suicide and was force-fed with a nasogastric intubation to keep her alive while in custody. In 2016 she ended her fast and said she would contest for elections in Manipur.

There have been other campaigns and efforts as well. Playful movements like the Pink Chaddi (pink underwear) campaign in 2009, when hundreds of women all over the country sent pink underwear to the headquarters of the Sri Ram Sena, an organisation that was going around moral policing by beating up women in pubs and threatening to force couples they found kissing on Valentine's Day to temples to be married. And the Gulabi Gang, or the pink gang, a large organisation of stick-wielding women in Uttar Pradesh who wear pink saris and go about beating rapists and demanding justice for victims.

The 2018 #MeToo campaign, while it didn't actually beat men up, did take judgement out of normal avenues of jurisdiction and unleashed an avalanche of stories from women around the country, leading to the downfall of several prominent men in the media and entertainment industry.

The most heartening sight I've seen recently, though, is the human chain of women created in Kerala in January 2019. Five million women gathered across

Above: Khuzani Devi, a farmer, in her house in the village of Bhagotipur in Haryana, a primarily agricultural state that is among the most conservative in India.

In/visible: A Woman's Place in India

Above: Lawyers Tanya Sanghvi and Shriya Prabhu
on the street near the High Court of Mumbai.

Above: Vrinda Dar, founder of the NGO Kautilya Society for the protection of the architectural heritage of Varanasi, sits in her residence and hostel Ram Bhawan, in the area of the city close to the ghats.

The Indian textiles industry is the world's second largest after that of China, and almost half of its exports go to the USA and the EU. The sector formally employs more than twelve million people, in addition to several million more in informal settings and at home, who are involved in various stages of production, from cutting sleeves to finishing work, such as adding embroidery, bows, fringes, beads and buttons. More than 90 per cent of these informal workers are female – some of them children – belonging mainly to minorities or marginalised groups such as the Dalit community and working in exploitative conditions. Wages are almost always a fraction of the legal minimum (as little as $0.15 an hour) and are often paid late or not at all. Harassment and intimidation by supervisors and managers is common, as is physical and psychological violence. Despite a government campaign to eliminate the use of child labour, it remains common; as is the so-called 'marriage scheme', in which girls aged between twelve and twenty-one are hired on three-year contracts with the promise of a final lump-sum payment to be used as a dowry (even though the practice of dowry payment is illegal). Few make it to the end of their contracts, however: exhausting shifts, severe curbs on their freedom of movement, accidents at work, disease and abuse force most workers to give up, and those who remain – unaware that board-and-lodging expenses are being deducted – often end up receiving less than the sum they were promised.

national highways creating a chain 620 kilometres long. The instigation for this outpouring was a Supreme Court judgement which passed a verdict allowing women to enter the Ayappa Temple in Sabarimala, Kerala, which for centuries had prevented women of menstruating age from entering the shrine for fear of enticing the residing bachelor deity. The law was hailed as progressive by the liberal left, but judiciary and society aren't always in step. The reality was that any woman who tried to enter the temple was blocked by devotees. Riots broke out, and one activist was killed. The women's wall rally was an act to support the court order and gender equality.

We are at an important intersection in India. The BJP government wants to move forward with the feeling of a world economic superpower, while half of the population still has no access to toilets. It wants to move towards a cash-free economy when half the population has no access to the internet or bank accounts.

For every victory there is a dark shadow of defeat. There may be all-female police stations, gender sensitisation campaigns in schools and workplaces, greater space in the media to report rape, but the fact is that twenty-seven million women are still stuck in the sex-trafficking business, and a religious leader like Asaram Bapu can suggest this as a rape preventative – that a woman who is getting raped only needs to call her rapist brother for it to stop.

We are looking at a future that is looking increasingly dystopic – villages where there will be no more women or girls, cities and centres that are ruled by men who enforce patriarchy at every turn. But we are also what Arundhati Roy called 'an irredeemably untidy people', and in this there is a possibility to stand up to the government and to patriarchy, 'in our diverse and untidy ways' (see 'Against Caste' by Arundhati Roy on page 109). I think of the hijras with whom I travelled so many years ago, who when they were harassed on the streets would lift up their skirts. This simple gesture of defiance, which brings it back to the body, to lift the skirt and say to the onlooker – take a look, what do you see there, dark hole, penis, woman, man? A way of diverting the terror to the onlooker. The way the Manipuri mothers deflected their rage on to the army by stripping naked. I think of a poem I wrote many years ago, imagining a river of all our lost Indian girls resurfacing from subterranean depths:

singing of a time in the universe
when they were born with tigers
breathing between their thighs;
when they set out for battle
with all three eyes on fire,
their golden breasts held high
like weapons to the sky.

How as long as we have our bodies we have resistance and there can be hope of recovery. 🐦

Rocket on a Bicycle

Mention of India's space programme, the ISRO, is rare in the West. If a film features a threat from space, it is always NASA that intervenes – or, at a push, Russia. Yet the ISRO impacts the lives of the subcontinent's entire population and, almost under the radar, it continues to work on grandiose projects.

SUSMITA MOHANTY

Left: Preparing to launch a rocket at the Thumba Equatorial Rocket Launching Station (TERLS), 1966. (© Henri Cartier-Bresson/ Magnum Photos/Contrasto)

HUMBLE BEGINNINGS

The story of the Indian space programme's humble beginnings has an almost endearing quality to it.

In the early days of our republic, Dr Vikram Sarabhai, a Cambridge-educated physicist and the scion of a wealthy mill-owning family who found his calling in nation building, went to convince Jawaharlal Nehru, the first prime minister, of the importance of a space programme for India. In Nehru he found a willing ally, and with government support Sarabhai founded the Indian Space Research Organisation (ISRO), India's equivalent of NASA.

In the early 1960s Sarabhai's team of scientists went scouting for a venue for their first experimental rocket launch. They settled on Thumba, a tiny fishing hamlet close to the earth's magnetic equator, in Trivandrum, the capital of the southern state of Kerala. On the beach in Thumba there was an old church, St Mary Magdalene, which the young scientists felt would make for a perfect place to have an office, a laboratory and a workshop to kick-start their adventures in space. Now all they had to do was persuade the bishop of Trivandrum to let them use the church as a home for the country's space mission. India's former president, the late Dr A.P.J. Abdul Kalam, himself a rocket scientist, recalled that the bishop encouraged his parishioners, mostly fisherfolk, to embrace the idea. First there was a nervous silence, followed by a hearty 'Amen' from the congregation. And thus, in a charming church, India's space programme was born.

The title of this piece is not fanciful. The legendary French photographer Henri Cartier-Bresson, whose then wife was good friends with the Nehru family, had unfettered access to chronicle a new nation in the making, and his iconic photo reproduced on page 48 is of a rocket cone actually being transported on a bicycle in Thumba. In those early days the young pioneers made do with what they could cobble together. Nothing would get in their way.

So, under the curious gaze of Mary Magdalene, the young scientists beavered away with the barest minimum of furniture and tools, building payloads and launching rockets. History was made with a US Nike-Apache – a small sounding (instrument-carrying) rocket – that ferried some French instruments into space on 21 November 1963, barely six years after the Soviet *Sputnik 1* merrily orbited the earth. This gives an idea of how early to the game the Indian space programme was.

A TALE OF TWO ROCKETS

India has come a long way since then. Not only did it start to build its own sounding rockets but it also went on to build bigger and more powerful ones. As one of the world's few launch-capable nations, India currently has two main rockets.

The smaller, the Polar Satellite Launch Vehicle (PSLV), is used to send remote-sensing (earth-observation) satellites into orbit. First launched in 1993, it is a very

SUSMITA MOHANTY is a spaceship designer and the only space entrepreneur in the world to have started companies on three different continents – MoonFront, San Francisco (2001–7), Liquifer, Vienna (2004–present) and Earth2Orbit, Bangalore (2009–present). Prior to turning entrepreneur she worked for the Space Station Program at Boeing in California and did a short stint at NASA. In 2019 Susmita was selected as one of the BBC's 100 Women laureates inspiring and influencing a female-led future. In 2017 she was featured on the cover of *Fortune* magazine. In 2016 she was nominated to the World Economic Forum Global Future Council for Space Technologies.

reliable, mature rocket in its class. In 2017 the PSLV achieved a world record when it launched 104 satellites in a single mission, breaking the previous record of thirty-seven satellites launched by Russia in 2014.

The bigger of the two is the Geosynchronous Satellite Launch Vehicle (GSLV), which, since 2001, has been used to launch heavy-tonnage communications satellites into geostationary orbit. The story surrounding the GSLV's cryogenic engine, which is central to its heavy-lift capabilities, reads like a classic cold-war-era tale of international intrigue. To get up to speed quickly, in the early 1990s India decided to procure the engines from the Russians, who were both willing to sell the engines to India *and* to transfer the technology required to manufacture them indigenously. The USA objected, citing this sharing of technology as a violation of the Missile Technology Control Regime – which seeks to minimise the risk of the proliferation of weapons of mass destruction and of which India, Russia and the USA are all members – and forced Russia to pull out of the deal. This and many other instances of arm-twisting by the USA are significant, because India, the world's largest democracy, is also one of its most pacifist: the country has fought no unprovoked wars, the last conflict being with Pakistan in 1971.

Repeated obstacles placed in the path of the Indian space programme by a world superpower would, however, do little to deter Indian scientists, who, with limited resources but unlimited resolve, would go on to craft a singular story of ingenuity and bring India to the forefront of the world's pre-eminent space nations.

TO VENTURE OR NOT TO VENTURE
Even today, half a century on from the first successful launch, I get asked, 'Why does India have a space programme when there

When the first man went to the moon in 1969 the only goal was to prove the USA's technological superiority. Since then just twelve people have left their footprints on the moon's surface, and no one has set foot there since 1972. Fifty years later, however, there is a renewed interest in space. The USA has announced that Americans will return to the moon in 2024, ahead of China, which has set a target of 2035. In the meantime, Japan, India, Russia and the EU are planning to flood the moon with robotic probes. Technological innovations and the resulting fall in costs, along with the ambitions of a new generation of entrepreneurs (Musk, Bezos and Branson, above all), mean that space is becoming ever more crowded. The promises of this new era include elite tourism and the development of communications networks, followed in the longer term by the exploitation of mineral reserves and even the colonisation of other planets. For the moment, however, the new space race is playing out closer to home, as the orbits of military and commercial satellites increasingly become an extension of the planet. Both China and India have already tested missiles against their own satellites, foreshadowing what could be the first steps of a potential war. As a consequence of this conflict scenario, satellites in the future will be cheaper, smaller and easier to launch into orbit. Soon, the traffic above our heads could be worse than the Delhi rush hour.

'Hollywood films have also played a definitive role in shaping the world's perception of who is at the top of the space totem pole. Caucasian male protagonists are a given. Aliens almost always touch down in the USA.'

are so many problems close to home that need solving?'

After India became a republic in 1950, Prime Minister Nehru, a modernist, made technology independence one of the country's top priorities. This new country, if it was ever to find its own footing, couldn't afford anything less. Sarabhai, the architect of the space programme, echoed these sentiments. 'There are some who question the relevance of space activities in a developing nation. To us, there is no ambiguity of purpose. We do not have the fantasy of competing with the economically advanced nations in the exploration of the moon or the planets or manned space flight. But we are convinced that if we are to play a meaningful role nationally, and in the community of nations, we must be second to none in the application of advanced technologies to the real problems of man and society.'

For the first four decades of ISRO's existence the focus was on developing indigenous capabilities for building spacecraft and using them for myriad applications to improve the lives of the Indian people. India's fleet of communications, earth-observation, meteorology and global-positioning satellites have become both an invisible and indivisible part of the everyday lives of millions of Indians. In the early years the focus was design and dissemination of educational programmes for farming and healthcare. Over the years the application portfolio has burgeoned to cover just about everything one can possibly imagine – television broadcasting, communications, cartography, disaster management, tele-education, tele-medicine, defence, urban planning, agriculture, forestry, logistics and more. India's space programme is, literally, embedded in our lives everywhere, and it has contributed mightily to our developmental goals.

Frequent hurricanes are a great example of how we use satellite data and meteorological models to predict cyclone parameters accurately, provide timely warning, evacuate and save millions of human lives. Loss of life in such events has decreased a hundred-fold in the last two decades (compare the number of deaths in the state of Odisha during a super-cyclone in 1999 – almost ten thousand – with the eighty-nine fatalities during the 2019 super-cyclone in the same region), and now Indian numbers are among the best in the world.

NO GUNPOWDER, NO ROCKETS
I was raised among the pioneers of the Indian space programme. While they were busy laying the groundwork, I was fortunate enough to have a ringside seat, and these formative years shaped my life's trajectory as a space architect and cross-border entrepreneur.

In 2007 I wrote to the legendary science-fiction author Arthur C. Clarke that I was planning to leave San Francisco and move back to India. Clarke wrote back saying: 'I think it is a *strategic* move.' I was surprised and asked him why he thought so. He said: 'Well, everything began in the east and it is going back there.' He cited the example of gunpowder, invented by

Chinese alchemists, and then quietly added: 'no gunpowder, no rockets'.

The success of eastern space powers such as India or China should come as no surprise for the enlightened mind. I sometimes get asked if there is a *space race* between India and China. Not really, I say, but if they insist on having the race, I refer them to the Aesop fable and tell them in jest, 'Well, yeah, China is the hare and India the tortoise.' China is the only nation to have landed on the moon in recent memory, once in December 2013 then in January 2019 and again in December 2020. The last time the Americans landed was in 1972 and the Soviets in 1976. India's attempt to soft land the *Chandrayaan-2* lander *Vikram* on the lunar surface in September 2019 was a failure, as was the Israeli attempt to land *Beresheet* a few months prior in February 2019.

A couple of years ago I got a call from a National Geographic producer who was looking for input for a mini-series to celebrate the fiftieth anniversary of that last Apollo landing in 1972. I asked her if she knew that, as we were speaking, a Chinese rover was pottering about on the moon. She seemed a little surprised. India and China are easily among the top space-faring nations of the world – the others being the USA, Russia, France and Japan – so when anyone refers to them as *emerging* space nations, I am amused. This ignorance stems from an entitled sense of misplaced Western superiority, historical amnesia and media stereotyping.

Hollywood films have also played a definitive role in shaping the world's perception of who is at the top of the space totem pole. Caucasian male protagonists are a given. Aliens almost always touch

down in the USA. Asteroids prefer cities like Paris or Los Angeles. The Russians are usually the bad guys. The Chinese space station is conveniently reduced to a pair of floating chopsticks. India doesn't really feature anywhere in the plots yet, but that is starting to change.

ORBITAL CHOREOGRAPHIES ON A SHOESTRING

ISRO has been chipping away for nearly five decades on organically evolving but grand goals, bit by bit, with practically zero hype. Public and political support has been rock steady. Mathematics, science and astronomy have been part of our civilisational narrative for centuries, so no surprises there. Indian rulers throughout history have often shown patronage in the development of fundamental knowledge. One grand example is the Jantar Mantar in Jaipur, commissioned by Maharajah Jai Singh II of Rajasthan. This cluster of mammoth architectural astronomical instruments, built in marble and sandstone in the early 1700s, is today a UNESCO heritage site.

As our resources dwindled – the result of two centuries of British colonial rule – some of that grandeur has given way to ingenuity. India's space programme, if anything, is a chronicle of that creativity and inventiveness. In August 2019

Page 53 and left: Jantar Mantar, an astronomical complex constructed in Delhi by Maharajah Jai Singh II around 1724 with the aim of compiling astronomical tables, calculating time and predicting the movement of the sun, moon and planets.

JAWAHARLAL NEHRU

In the wake of Jawaharlal Nehru's death in 1964 an article in *The Economist* celebrated him as a man who, in the battle for India's modernisation and independence, had unsuspectingly paved the way for the rest of the developing world. Nehru was an unusual figure. Born into an upper-class family, he studied law in Britain but abandoned the legal profession for politics. He entered the Indian National Congress and advocated socialist policies, influenced by visits to Europe and the Soviet Union. A key encounter came in 1916, when he met Mohandas Gandhi, becoming his secular counterpart: in the 1920s and 1930s he took part in the Home Rule independence movement and the non-cooperation movement, leading to his imprisonment on several occasions for civil disobedience. He was elected president of the Congress Party in 1929 and adhered to the principles of anti-fascism and the right of nations to self-determination. His protests against Britain's decision to involve India in the Second World War led to his arrest, as did his participation in the Quit India campaign. In 1947, in a country rocked by conflict between Hindus and Muslims, Nehru pushed for Partition as the only chance for peace, and on 15 August that year he assumed the office of prime minister of an independent India, which he held until his death. In addition to a scientific model of resource management, his policies were informed by a focus on industrialisation, and the creation of the space programme is a perfect example of this.

Above: Visitors to the National Science Centre, Delhi, watch a 3D film on the exploration of space.
Below: Models of the rockets used by ISRO, India's space programme, at the National Science Centre.

ISRO pulled off its second lunar mission, *Chandrayaan-2*, on a budget of less than $150 million, a fraction of what a major Hollywood blockbuster would cost today. Rather than muscle our way to the moon in a couple of days by launching a mega-rocket straight at it, ISRO scientists did something clever. They traded off forty-eight days of time. The extra time it would take to reach the moon was completely worth it for vast cost savings and a major nod to the environment. They designed a sophisticated orbital choreography around the earth and used the moon's gravity to capture *Chandrayaan-2* into its orbit.

Another ISRO mission that caught the world's imagination was India's debut mission to the red planet in 2013 – *Mangalyaan-1*, aka the Mars Orbiter Mission – when India became the first country ever to make it to Mars on the first attempt. Yet again, we achieved this ambitious mission on a shoestring. *Mangalyaan-1* was achieved in a record time – a mere fifteen months after the budget approval came in; typically, planetary missions take six or seven years. ISRO's space endeavours are a picture of quiet efficiency, agility and adaptive thinking – traits that are missing in larger space agencies that enjoy plentiful resources.

Popular imagination has now caught up with the Indian space programme – enough to inspire a Bollywood film, *Mission Mangal*, loosely based on our Mars mission. *Mission Mangal* turned out to be one of the biggest blockbusters of 2019.

ROCKET WOMEN

Mangalyaan-1 also catapulted ISRO to social-media glory because a photograph of ISRO women scientists in silk saris and flowers in their hair celebrating the success went viral. ISRO has one of the best gender ratios of any space agency. The Mangalyaan team comprised five hundred scientists from ten ISRO centres, with a third of the key executive positions held by women. For *Chandrayaan-2*, the mission director, Ritu Karidhal, and project director, M. Vanitha, were both women. Another ISRO woman scientist who has been in the spotlight lately is Dr V.R. Lalithambika; she is leading ISRO's Gaganyaan mission that will launch humans into space by 2022.

As someone with an interest in the names of space missions, I have always been a fan of Japanese and Russian choices, but our names are pretty good, too. We call our Mars missions Mangalyaan and lunar missions Chandrayaan; the human missions will be called Gaganyaan. The word *yaan* means a vehicle, a transporter, in Sanskrit; *mangal* is Mars, *chandra* is the moon, *gagan* is the sky.

THE STARS ARE CALLING

Remember Edmund Hillary and Tenzing Norgay, the duo who first reached the summit of Everest in 1953? Hillary was a wealthy New Zealander while Tenzing was a Sherpa high-altitude porter; both were intrepid mountaineers from different economic backgrounds. But, like climbing Everest, travelling to Mars isn't just about mission economics but also about the shared human drive to push boundaries, to endure, to achieve the impossible. Time after time, without much fanfare, ISRO has made major leaps. Not to explore is to deny ourselves even the possibility of success.

India has a very young demographic, with nearly 65 per cent of our population under the age of thirty-five. The optimism, the boldness that our space programme embodies, gives our youth something to dream about, to dare, to seek, to transcend existential goals. As good old Oscar Wilde rightly said: 'We are all in the gutter, but some of us are looking at the stars.' ✦

Farmers set fire to their fields following the rice harvest in the Haryana countryside near Bhagotipur village.

The Monsoon: A Gamble on the Rains

THE ECONOMIST

The monsoon rains have held sway over agriculture and life in the planet's most populous region since the earliest times. But how, why and where do they form, what effects do they have – and, crucially, what of the future? A story of famines, business, science and greed.

With rheumy eyes and a face wizened by the sun, Narayanappa looks down to the ground and then, slowly, up to the skies. After weeks of harsh heat his land, one and a half hectares of peanuts, chillies and mulberry bushes, has turned to dust. At the beginning of June 2019 a dozen families local to Kuppam, a village in the Chittoor district of the south-eastern state of Andhra Pradesh, came together, as they do every year, to sacrifice a goat as a divine down payment on a good monsoon. By mid-June the monsoon rains should be quenching the parched ground. Yet there is no sign of the livid clouds running up from the south-eastern horizon which serve as its evening harbingers, rising and churning, filling the sky with their rumbling and the night with veiled lightning. The sky is as blank as the ground is dry. Narayanappa has his sacks of nuts ready to sow. But time is running out.

In his office at the India Meteorological Department in New Delhi, Madhavan Nair Rajeevan, the department's boss, looks at portents which are dry in a different way – figures and lines on paper and screens. Where once the oncoming monsoon was spotted through telescopes on the veranda of the observatory built by the Maharajah of Travancore on a hill above Thiruvananthapuram (formerly Trivandrum) in Kerala, now the signs of its coming are looked for through tracked radar and satellites. But they are still of intense interest to the country's rulers and its people. The monsoon's arrival in Thiruvananthapuram at the beginning of June marks the official beginning of India's rainy season. The rains' subsequent movement is tracked on a daily basis by national television stations, rather like the advance of the spring cherry blossom in Japan but with far greater human consequence.

A century of meteorological progress means that Mr Rajeevan can say with much more confidence than his predecessors how fast the summer monsoon will sweep up the nation and how much rain, overall, it will bring. When the monsoon started late he could give a convincing non-goat-related reason: a cyclone in the Arabian Sea, which upset the flows on which the monsoon depends. But, though meteorology has improved, it has a long way to go. On average the monsoon is a regular wave of rain, rising and falling over the months from June to September. In any given year, though, the smooth wave is overwritten by spikes and troughs, bursts of intense precipitation and weeks of odd dryness, variations known as 'vagaries' which science still struggles to grasp.

There is a complex structure in space as well as time. Some places may be almost completely skirted by the rains; others see deluges violent enough to destroy crops and carry away soil, the water running off the land before it can be caught and stored. The flooding that goes with such rains is expected to become worse and wider spread as the global climate warms. Agriculture remains the Indian economy's largest source of jobs, directly accounting for a sixth of its GDP and employing almost half of its working people. A bad monsoon

'Agriculture remains the Indian economy's largest source of jobs, directly accounting for a sixth of its GDP and employing almost half of its working people.'

can knock Indian economic growth by a third. The effects in Bangladesh, Bhutan, Nepal, Pakistan and Sri Lanka are on a similar scale. Almost a quarter of the world – 1.76 billion souls – lives with the South Asian monsoon.

As Guy Fleetwood Wilson, a finance minister, put it in 1909, the 'budget of India is a gamble in rain'. Thanks to Mr Rajeevan and his colleagues, the odds of each year's gamble are now better known. But obvious steps that might lower the stakes being played for are still not taken. Storage systems in cities have fallen into disuse; aquifers under farmland are depleted year by year faster than the monsoons can refill them. In a country where more people will face the risks of climate change in the decades to come than any other, the problems of the current climate are being ducked.

The metamorphosis brought by the burst of the monsoon is profound. Brown landscapes turn green, dusts become muds, cracks turn into mouths through which the earth slakes its thirst. The Ganges and the other great rivers fill then overflow, spreading silt-rich fertility across their floodplains. In the countryside the air takes up the petrichor aroma of fresh earth. In gardens, the scent of frangipani carries on the damp breeze; in cities, that unmistakably Indian blend of ordure, asphalt and spice.

The people respond. The rains bring a sense of relief and a new sensuality. In 'The Cloud Messenger' by Kalidasa, one of the greatest Sanskrit poets of north India, the meeting of earth and clouds is nothing less than a kind of lovemaking. In the Sangam literature of the deep south, the heroine waits for her lover, who is away seeking war, wealth and adventure, to return with the rains. People still tell stories of inhibitions cast aside and new lovers taken. The heart takes on the driving, unpredictable rhythms of the rain.

For all its complexity and importance, on every scale from that of smallholders to empires, at its heart the monsoon is something fairly simple: a season-long version of the sea breezes familiar to all those who live by coasts. Because land absorbs heat faster than water, on a sunny day the land and the air above it warm faster than adjoining seas. The hot air rises; the cooler air from above the sea blows in to take its place.

A monsoon is the same sort of phenomenon on a continental scale. As winter turns to summer, the Indian subcontinent warms faster than the waters around it. Rising hot air means low pressure; moist maritime water is drawn in to fill the partial void. This moist water, too, rises, and, as it does, its water vapour condenses, releasing both water, to fall as rain, and energy to drive further convection, pulling up yet more moist air from below.

There are other monsoonal circulations around the world – in Mexico and the American south-west and in West Africa, as well as in East Asia, to the circulation of which the South Asian monsoon is conjoined. But geography makes the South Asian monsoon particular in a number of ways. The Indian Ocean, unlike the Pacific and the Atlantic, does not stretch up into the Arctic. This means that water warmed

SUMMER

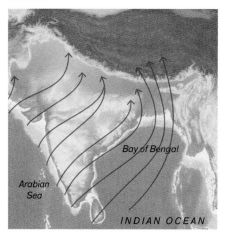

WINTER

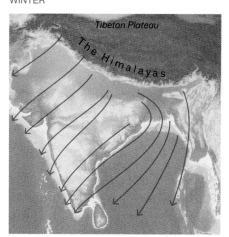

SOURCE: NOAA EARTH SYSTEM RESEARCH LABORATORY

in the tropical regions cannot just flow north, taking its heat with it. It stays in the Arabian Sea and the Bay of Bengal, lapping at India from the west and the east. And to the subcontinent's north sits the Tibetan plateau, the highest on the planet. The summer heat there draws the monsoon's moisture far higher into the atmosphere than it would otherwise be able to go, adding mountains of cloud to the Himalayan peaks.

The monsoon is thus a mixture of necessity and chance. Given the arrangement of sea and land and the flow of heat from equator to pole, such a season has to exist; given the vagaries of weather from year to year, and within the seasons themselves, it springs surprises for good and ill. It is also, and increasingly, a mixture of the natural and the human – as evermore humans depend on it, as humans learn new ways

of anticipating it and as humans face up to the climate change that will reshape it.

THE WINDS THAT MADE ASIA

The rains for which Narayanappa waits are not the whole story. The word 'monsoon' blew into English from Portuguese in the late 16th century, not because European sailors cared about the rain on alien plains but because when they followed Vasco da Gama around the tip of Africa they came across a type of wind they had never encountered and for which they had no name.

The Portuguese *monção* comes in its turn from the Arabic *mawsim*, which means 'season'. In the Atlantic Ocean, the only one to which the Portuguese were accustomed, winds in any given place tend to blow in pretty much the same direction throughout the year, though their intensities

SUMMER

① Evaporation ③ Temperature drops
② Formation of clouds ④ Air returns

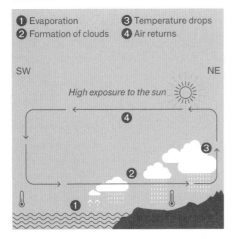

WINTER

① Descending wind (temperature rises)
② Air returns

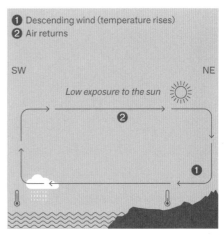

SOURCE: KIT KARLSRUHE INSTITUTE OF TECHNOLOGY

change with the season and their prevailing direction changes with the latitude. In the Indian Ocean the prevailing winds flip back and forth. This is because of the role played in the monsoon by the 'intertropical convergence zone' (ITCZ) which encircles the world close to the equator. The ITCZ is a zone of low pressure over the warmest water. In all the oceans this low pressure draws in steady winds from the south-east known as the southern trade winds.

During the northern hemisphere's winter, the ITCZ sits south of the equator in the Indian Ocean. As warmth creeps north, so does the ITCZ, becoming a dynamic part of the monsoon. It ends up nestled against the Himalayas, bringing the southern trades with it. But their move from the southern hemisphere to the northern, and the constraining effect of high pressure over Africa, sees them twisted from

south-easterlies to south-westerlies. When these south-westerly trades pick up in late spring – wind speeds in the Arabian Sea can double over a few weeks – the rains are on their way to Thiruvananthapuram.

Just as coastal breezes turn around at set of sun, when the land cools fast and the sea stays warm, so monsoons reverse in winter. This is true both for the South Asian monsoon and the East Asian monsoon, which affects Indo-China, the Philippines, southern China, Taiwan, Korea and part of Japan. As the land cools in the autumn, north-easterly winds replace the south-westerlies. Because the winds are mostly dry they are not so important to farmers, though they do bring rain to some parts of southern India. But they matter a great deal to navigation and thus to human history. The monsoon rains feed what has always been the most populous

part of the human world. It is the monsoon winds, though, which brought those people together to form Asia.

Winds which reverse with the seasons shaped a maritime world stretching from the Strait of Hormuz in the north-west to the island archipelagos of South East Asia, from Madagascar in the south-west to Japan. With patience, this whole world could be traversed in both directions, with vessels set fair for east and north in summer, west and south in the winter – and with layovers enforced by the tropical storms called hurricanes in the Atlantic, typhoons in East Asia and cyclones in the Indian Ocean (the term comes from the Greek *kukloma*, the coil of a serpent). The winds of the South Asian monsoon suppress the conditions needed for cyclones to form. When the monsoon is over, they come out to play.

It was a world of long-range trade where seafarers mingled quite freely. And India sat athwart it. Before any written record, the Bay of Bengal was the realm of floating communities of water nomads, with mastery of the seas and little sense of bounded space. Their boat-dwelling descendants live on as the Moken, Orang Suku Laut and Bajau Laut. Today they are marginalised, subjected to ever-tightening pressure by the state to respect borders and come ashore. Long ago they showed others what lay over the horizon.

Had sailors, traders and holy men not followed their lead on the monsoon winds, Asia would not be the heterogeneous place it has been through history – and remains today, despite the nationalist narratives and more strictly bordered lives its

20th-century states forced on their newly minted citizens. Tamil merchants from southern India put up inscribed stones in Burma (modern-day Myanmar) and Thailand around the 7th century CE. They seem to have reached the southern Chinese emporium of Canton (Guangzhou) not much later. India's influence is intense in the extraordinary 9th-century Buddhist temple of Borobudur on Java. Hindu kingdoms arose in the Indonesian archipelago. Bali represents surely the most embellished version of the Hindu faith today. Via India, Islam spread east, too, after Arab merchants carried their faith to the Malabar Coast of south-west India and, eventually, to Quanzhou on China's eastern seaboard, where 13th-century Muslims lie beneath gravestones inscribed in Arabic. Later, with the Portuguese, Roman Catholicism came to Goa and then, via the south China coast, to Japan.

Arabs, East Africans, Bengalis, Tamils, Parsees, Malays, Chinese, 'Manila men' (Filipinos) and Okinawans met and traded, sometimes sojourning in each other's lands, sometimes returning on the next season's winds. When European merchant venturers – Portuguese, Dutch, French and British – came to the region they joined in these seasonal rhythms. The East India Company put the monsoon winds to the service of joint-stock capitalism, as 'East Indiamen', heavily armed merchant ships, carried Indian silks and cottons as well as Chinese tea back to Europe once a year.

In the 19th century, with the coming of coal, steam and iron, the Europeans broke with seasonal rhythms, establishing colonial dominance over Asia by means of efficient weaponry and Suez-crossing steamships that could defy the wind to allow a constant flow of raw materials one way – cotton, jute, grain, timber, tin – and returned manufactures the other.

The sugarcane harvest
near Bhagotipur.

The Asian ports established or greatly expanded at the time – Bombay (present-day Mumbai), Calcutta (Kolkata), Madras (Chennai), Batavia (Jakarta), Manila, Shanghai – marked the birth of a fossil-fuel age. The winds were forgotten; but they were not unchanged. As the build up of atmospheric greenhouse gases which began back then traps evermore heat, the monsoons will change; the vast clouds of pollutants created by Asia's now endemic use of coal and oil are affecting them, too, in ways that meteorologists do not yet understand. And those great low-lying colonial ports will prove far more susceptible to sudden flooding and rises in sea level than older, more defensible ports further up rivers were. The ninety million inhabitants of Asia's great seaboard cities are among the most vulnerable to the Industrial Revolution's longest legacy.

SEEING LIKE AN EMPIRE
Just a few hundred kilometres from Narayanappa's smallholding in Chittoor lie the deltas of the Godavari and the Krishna. India's second- and fourth-longest rivers respectively, they rise in the Western Ghats and flow east into the Bay of Bengal. The contrast between straitened Chittoor, at the mercy of its own local rains, and the verdant deltas could not be starker. Water drawn from the rivers and spread across their deltas allows the lowland farmers to raise two crops a year, sometimes three. Satellite pictures show their lush paddy fields of the delta as emerald patches on the brown scrub of the Coromandel Coast and the land behind. It is a lesson in the power of water to make or break and the power of humans to command it.

The green of the deltas was not always so reliable. William Roxburgh was a surgeon who left Edinburgh in 1772 to join the East India Company. He settled in Samulcottah (modern-day Samalkota) in the Godavari delta. As Sunil Amrith writes in *Unruly Waters* (Basic Books USA/Penguin UK), a fascinating history of the monsoon, Roxburgh was one of those who, through measured observation, laid the foundations of modern Indian meteorology. In so doing he came to believe that nature in India was capable of much 'improvement'. The Godavari's cultivators, he pointed out, depended entirely on the rains: 'when they fail, a famine is, and must ever be the consequence'. The solution was to harness the water that 'passes annually unemployed into the sea', retaining it for farmers' year-round use.

The British were far from the first of the rulers of the Indian subcontinent to transform the hydraulic landscape. The water tank known as the Great Bath of Mohenjo-Daro is part of an urban complex built by rulers of the Indus valley civilisation in the third millennium BCE. In 1568 CE Akbar, the third Mughal emperor, had water brought to Delhi not only to 'supply the wants of the poor' but also to 'leave permanent marks of the greatness of my empire'. He did so by restoring and enlarging a canal to the river Yamuna first cut two centuries earlier by a 14th-century sultan. Akbar's works, in turn, were restored and re-engineered by the British two and a half centuries later.

Yet no illustrious ruler had turned his attention to the Godavari. Its improvement fell instead to an unassuming engineer from Dorking in Surrey, Arthur Cotton. Thousands of Indian labourers working under his direction built a giant barrage at Dowleswaram, regulating the river's flow through the use of huge gates described at the time as 'the noblest feat of engineering skill which has yet been accomplished in British India'. To this day, local people lionise Cotton *dora* ('Boss' Cotton) for

'If India's Victorian rulers were happy to lay a restraining hand on the subcontinent's rivers, they were chillingly unwilling to interrupt the free markets they imposed on it.'

turning the delta into India's rice bowl. On his birthday farmers hang garlands on his statue.

But if India's Victorian rulers were happy to lay a restraining hand on the subcontinent's rivers, they were chillingly unwilling to interrupt the free markets they imposed on it. Growing cash crops for distant markets uprooted old community patterns of mutual obligation during periods of rain-starved stress. In the late 19th century terrible famines linked to failed monsoons took tens of millions of lives in Asia.

In 1876 and 1877, when the summer rains failed completely, India's administrators invoked the authority of Adam Smith to argue against intervening in the famine, which began to spread across the dry land, eventually claiming 5.5 million lives (some estimates say the total was far higher). A couple of years earlier, during a local drought in Bihar, a major catastrophe had been averted through imports of rice from Burma. Yet such expenditure on relief had met with much criticism, not least from *The Economist* itself. Such an approach, we wrote, would encourage lazy Indians to believe that 'it is the duty of the Government to keep them alive'.

When famine spread in 1877 the viceroy, Lord Lytton, was determined that such folly should not be repeated. He vehemently opposed district officers' attempts to stockpile grain on the basis that it would distort the market. The railways, built with the help of taxes that had impoverished the now starving peasants, ensured that grain could get to where it would fetch the highest price – for

example, by being exported to Britain – rather than stay in place, unprofitably saving lives. The administration cut both relief rations and the wage for a punishing day's work in the relief camps, limiting the victims' access to markets yet further.

A century later Amartya Sen, a Nobel-winning economist, argued that what happened in the 1870s was the rule not the exception: governments are the general cause of famine. Mass starvation is not brought about by a crop-disease- or climate-driven absolute lack of food but by policies and hierarchies which stop people from exchanging their primary 'entitlement', in Mr Sen's terms – for instance, their labour – for what food there is. Such policies are a feature of autocracies; where the entitlements of the people include real political power, as they do in functioning democracies, they are normally untenable. It was an academic insight born of childhood witness. As a child Mr Sen lived through the Bengal famine of 1943, during which Indians died in the street in front of well-stocked shops guarded by the British state.

That famine, in which up to three million Bengalis perished, followed a devastating cyclone. But much of the damage was done by the scorched-earth policy of colonial officials who, fearing a Japanese invasion, burned the vessels that local cultivators used to ship rice. Britain sent no relief – in part, perhaps, because of Winston Churchill's active dislike of Indians agitating for independence. Jawaharlal Nehru, who would later become India's first prime minister but was at the time imprisoned by the British, wrote from jail 'that in any democratic or semi-democratic country, such a calamity would have swept away all the governments concerned with it'. Though India has experienced plenty of droughts and food shortages since independence, it has suffered no tragedy on a scale to compare with those of the late 19th and early 20th centuries.

If the Raj was indifferent as to the human effects of failed monsoons, though, it did exhibit an interest in the failures' causes. In the early 20th century Gilbert Walker, a brilliant Cambridge mathematician who became director of the India Meteorological Department Mr Rajeevan now runs, set his large staff of Indian 'computers' to analysing weather data from around the world in search of patterns. His breakthrough came when he perceived back and forths even grander than that of the winds over the Indian Ocean – co-ordinated changes in pressure in places many thousands of kilometres apart which he called 'world weather'.

One of these features was the Southern Oscillation. The usual pattern of air pressure over the Pacific features high pressure over Tahiti and low pressure over Darwin in northern Australia. This dispensation helps drive the trade winds westwards the better to feed the monsoon as the inter-tropical convergence zone sweeps north over India. But a few times a decade a reversal takes place: the pressure that was up goes down, and that which was down goes up. Low pressure over Tahiti and high pressure over Darwin disrupts the trade winds. The South Asian monsoon weakens.

Walker guessed that the flipping back and forth had to do with 'variations in activity of the general oceanic circulation'; but he did not know what they were, and the atmospheric correlations, though real, proved insufficient to the task of improving forecasts of the monsoon. The rest of the puzzle was solved by Jacob Bjerknes, a Norwegian at the University of California, Los Angeles, in 1969. In the tropical Pacific the eastern waters off South America tend to be cooler than the western ones. Periodically, though, the waters of the east warm while those of the west get cooler. It is this which causes Walker's seesaw to tip. But the atmosphere in its turn influences the ocean. The strength of the easterly winds in the Pacific is one of the factors that governs distribution of warmth between the east and west. The winds and the oceans operate as a 'coupled system', with heat and momentum shifting from one to the other and back again.

This coupled system has, since Bjerknes, been known as ENSO: EN for El Niño, the name that Peruvians give to warm waters around Christmas time; SO for the Southern Oscillation. There are other regular oscillations in the planet's climate, but ENSO is by far the most important one. When ENSO shifts in the warm-water-off-Peru direction, known as its positive phase, warmth stored in the waters of the Pacific flows into the atmosphere, warming the whole globe. The changes are felt not just in the Pacific and India but around the tropics and to some extent beyond. When ENSO is in its positive phase, drought can be expected in parts of southern Africa and eastern Brazil, too, while the southern United States can expect things to be wet. In the negative phase – La Niña – the situation is largely reversed.

The advent of computerised global-climate models capable of capturing the effects of far-flung changes in sea-surface temperature at a reasonable level of detail has in the past decade given Walker's heirs more confidence in predicting the South Asian monsoon's relative strength. It has also underscored the complexity of the

Ratio of total water consumption
to total water supply

Low (<10%)
Low–medium (10–20%)
Medium–high (20–40%)
High (40–80%)
Extremely high (>80%)

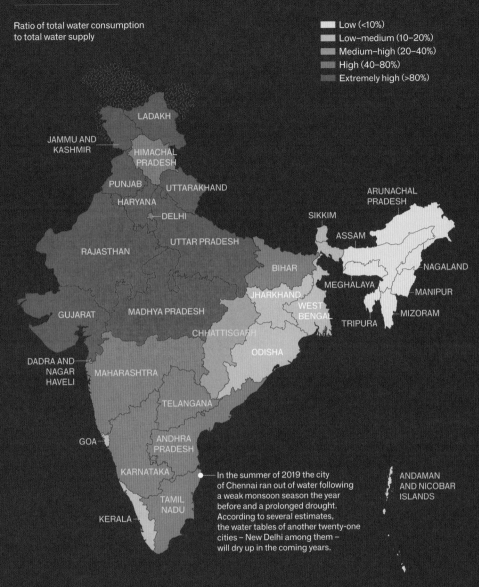

In the summer of 2019 the city
of Chennai ran out of water following
a weak monsoon season the year
before and a prolonged drought.
According to several estimates,
the water tables of another twenty-one
cities – New Delhi among them –
will dry up in the coming years.

600

million people are facing 'high'
or 'extremely high' levels of water
stress and are vulnerable
to uncertainties like drought
and massive water consumption.

75%

of families don't have a supply
of drinking water at home; 84%
of families in rural areas don't have
running water.

70%

of the water supply in the country
is contaminated; India is in 120th
place out of 122 in the world
water-quality index.

SOURCE: WORLD RESOURCES INSTITUTE

'It is now clear that the failures of the monsoon in the late 19th century were due to very powerful super El Niños. Some climate models suggest that these will occur more often in a warming world.'

climate system and its interactions with human history. It is now clear that the failures of the monsoon which the British exacerbated in the late 19th century were due to very powerful super El Niños. Some climate models suggest that these will occur more often in a warming world. Others, though, disagree. Climate modelling has improved understanding of the monsoon from year to year, but if you take the models which best capture the effects of ENSO in the 20th century and ask what they have to say about how it will work in the hotter 21st century, you find no consensus.

BREAKS AND VAGARIES

There is one thing the locals do not talk about in the wettest place on earth: the rain. What, ask the townsfolk of Mawsynram, is the point?

Their settlement sits on a hilltop plateau in the north-eastern state of Meghalaya – 'abode of the clouds'. Immediately to the south, the hills fall away to Bangladesh's steaming plains nearly 1,500 metres below in a sharply picturesque way – 'Danger: Selfie Zone' a road sign warns. To the north are the Khasi Hills, standing athwart the path of moisture-laden southerly winds eager to continue north. The hills scoop the wet air upwards, wringing out its rain.

The consequence, in Mawsynram, is daily rain for a good nine months of the year. The settlement sees 11.9 metres of rainfall in an average year, over a dozen times that seen in Manchester, say, or

Seattle: in an exceptional year it can see sixteen metres. Before the monsoon it comes in heavy night-time thunderstorms. From late May it is nearly continuous, sometimes a steady drizzle, sometimes rods that rattle tin roofs too loudly for conversation. Why a tin roof? Dead wood rots quickly, so the locals often build with metal – or with wood that is still alive, training the aerial roots of *Ficus elastica*, the rubber fig, to form bridges over the rivers and streams by which the water flows down to the plains below.

The certainty of daily rain, though, marks Mawsynram out as unusual. In most places there is a great deal of variation in rainfall over the course of the monsoon. The season is marked by prominent 'active' spells, typically when depressions travel west along the monsoon front, followed by dry 'breaks'. Timing the sowing of a successful crop is a gamble on what breaks may come, and for how long. Yet today's meteorological models remain poor at predicting the monsoon's weather more than a few days out.

Then comes the need for more localised predictions. Knowing where storms will do their worst would save not just crops but lives: lightning kills more Indians than cyclones do, though cyclones do much more damage to property. Monsoon meteorology's big challenge, then, is to improve predictions of these intraseasonal shifts. That means combining its models of global climate with an understanding of local peculiarity. The source of much of that can be found in the source of the rains that roll down the Khasi Hills: the Bay of Bengal.

Thanks to satellite imagery and cloud-busting radar, R. Venkatesan of the National Institute of Ocean Technology in Chennai points out, people now know pretty well what is happening in the atmosphere. But 'the ocean remains very murky'. His high-roofed warehouse in Chennai is a treasure trove of toys dedicated to demurkifying it: instrument-laden, unmanned sea kayaks for taking surface measurements; buoys that anchor to the sea bed with sensors to measure temperature, salinity and current; autonomous floats that drift about collecting data at the surface and at depth; an engineless underwater 'glider' that soars through the water column, surfacing every few days to tell satellites what it has gleaned. Many of them are about to be deployed in the Bay of Bengal.

The bay, the world's biggest, has a notable oddity. It boasts a distinct surface layer of light, comparatively fresh water floating on top of its deep-sea salinity. This layer is maintained by two things: one is the Brahmaputra, the Ganges and the rest of the lesser rivers, such as the Godavari and the Krishna, that drain most of the subcontinent's rainfall into the sea to its east; the other is rain that falls on to the bay itself. This fresher water means the top few metres of the bay are much less well mixed than is the norm in oceans – and thus that the sea-surface temperature can vary more quickly. This thermodynamic skittishness is passed on to the air above.

In 2015 a joint US–Indian mission used Mr Venkatesan's hardware, among other tools, to study interactions between the bay and the weather in unprecedented detail. The study reinforced the scientists' belief that the bay's quick changes are the key to the breaks between monsoon rains. Rain falling on to the bay itself cools the surface layer enough to limit the convection that would produce more rain for a while before the surface heats back up again. A follow-on mission was designed to refine the analysis by gathering real-time temperature, salinity, current and wind data to put together a better picture of how the Bay of Bengal makes the weather, propagating bursts and hiatuses.

Meanwhile, in the Khasi Hills, pepper gardens and betel-leaf plots on the hillsides will go untended as the rain pours down. Instead, people will lend their hands to the rain's long-term project of dismantling the hills themselves. In recent years local kingpins have been putting the industrious locals to new work: felling the hills' forests to get at the coal, limestone, China clay and even gold underneath. An orgy of illegal quarrying and 'rat-hole' mining is disfiguring the landscape and eroding the hillsides and stream beds. Khasi men and women sit by roadsides with ball-peen hammers reducing boulders to pebbles the size of peas that will descend to the plains not by stream but by lorry, there to feed an infrastructure boom on the alluvial plains of Bangladesh.

Damaging and unsightly though it may be locally, the mining and quarrying is small beer compared with the work of nature. All the sediments in the plains where the Bangladeshis are building come from hills and mountains eroded away by winter ice, springtime melts and monsoon rains for tens of millions of years. But if humans are not all that impressive on the mountain-levelling-plains-building side of things, they more than make up for it when it comes to inundating the plains with ever greater bursts of flooding and washing them away with sea-level rise – processes which will have consequences for that infrastructure boom in far fewer than a million years.

BOTTOMED-OUT WELL

Agrasen ki Baoli – 'Agrasen's step well' – is one of Delhi's oldest structures. It was built (or perhaps rebuilt) in the 14th century by followers of a mythical king whose life is chronicled in the earliest Sanskrit epics. The country is covered with a vast number of water tanks and step wells, some of them stunningly elaborate, used variously for irrigation, drinking water and religious purification. Thus contained, water signifies political and religious power – as well as life itself.

Yet today the bottom of Agrasen ki Baoli is just dust. That might be read as testament to the heatwave and drought by which much of India has remained gripped as the monsoon stalls in the southern states of Kerala and Tamil Nadu. Recently, when this correspondent climbed down to the step well's bottom, Delhi's temperature hit forty-eight degrees Centigrade in the shade.

But it is all too tempting to view the empty *baoli* as a metaphor for decades of human folly in which precious water in India has been squandered. Some forty years ago, when the *baoli* was still full, a farming transformation was under way – a 'green revolution' marrying new seed varieties with artificial fertilisers and pesticides. Just add water. The *baoli*'s builders would have been amazed at how crop yields soared. They would have been appalled at the green revolution's other consequences, which include soil erosion, a plundering of aquifers and toxic water in much depleted water tables.

THE HUMAN STREAM

They would also have been appalled to see how urban development has outrun the wells and rivers. Just one instance: in late June 2019 Chennai, India's sixth-biggest city, was officially declared to have run out of water. Its municipal authorities blamed the drought. Yet years ago they abandoned any coherent policy of water supply. Not only did they not factor in new water capacity or conservation measures they allowed developers to fill in the water tanks and seasonal lakes for which the city was once famous. The towers of gated communities now rise on these lake beds. A giant billboard outside one such development, Golden Opulence, in Chennai's western exurbs, promises well-heeled buyers limitless water as a chief sales pitch. The supply is guaranteed by the tankers of a well-established 'water mafia' whose thousands of soot-belching lorries are a continuous threat to the city's air, pedestrians and cyclists. Their cargo disgorged, they return to the countryside – specifically, to places where farmers lucky enough to sit on top of an aquifer replenish them for city cash. For farmers wealthy enough to drill a bore hole and install an electric pump this is a doddle, not least because electricity for farmers is essentially free. Mining water beats farming crops.

Narayanappa, in Chittoor district, has no such scam to support him. The butterflies enjoying the shade of the well he dug in the 1990s flit over a stagnant puddle. He and his family have borrowed from local moneylenders to drill five bore holes across the smallholding. Four of them, including the one which goes down 460 metres, are now dry. And even in better years than this one, bore-well water is not always sweet or safe to drink, given levels of naturally

Right: A farmer winnowing rice in the countryside near Rohtak, Haryana.

From the Himalayas to the Bay of Bengal, the Ganges runs for 2,525 kilometres through five of India's most populous states. For the 400 million Indians who live within its basin, it is a source of sustenance, water and energy as well as a means of transport. To Hindus the river is also a goddess, worshipped with offerings of flowers and food. The water of the sacred river not only purifies those who immerse themselves in it or drink it but is also said to purify itself. And yet the Ganges is one of the world's most polluted rivers: around eleven billion litres of industrial effluent are released into its waters every day. The decline sets in not far from its headwaters, with diversion channels and hydroelectric power plants that release floods or trickles of water depending on the season and the demands of the grid. The real pollution begins as it flows through urban areas, where sewage and rubbish are carried into the river each time there is heavy rainfall. But there are two main critical points: the first is Kanpur, with its tanning industry, which is almost entirely in Muslim hands (along with the Dalits, they are the only people able to process the hides of cows, held sacred by Hindus); the other is Varanasi, the spiritual centre of Hinduism, where discharges have turned the river into an open sewer in which the level of faecal coliform bacteria is at least three thousand times WHO standards. Since 1986 various governments have spent hundreds of millions of dollars on cleaning the river up, but the money has often been swallowed up by corruption and wasteful spending. The latest and most ambitious project, entitled Namami Gange, was launched by Prime Minister Modi in 2014, mobilising $2.9 billion from public and private funds, but the results are slow in coming.

occurring arsenic. For the past five years the water tankers have been coming to farms around Kuppam village, too.

The gamble on the rains is not just for finance ministers. If, despite ENSO and cyclones, the monsoon comes good, as Mr Rajeevan thinks it will, Narayanappa wins out, sells his crops, repays his debts. If not, he goes deeper into hock. The desperation such debt drives has led to protests – some violent – and suicide. The misery is one example of how water and the want of water determine inequalities and even fates. Another can be seen in attacks on people of lower caste using water tanks customarily monopolised by the upper castes. There are also water wars between states. These phenomena are not new – the bitter dispute between Karnataka and Tamil Nadu over extracting water from the river Cauvery dates back to the 1890s – but they speak poorly of modern India's ability to manage the stakes in its monsoonal roulette.

At the far end of Narayanappa's land runs the railway from Mumbai to the south. To the old folk of the village the crammed carriages rolling past are another world, one that fleetingly flows through theirs a few times a day. When the rains fail, their children and grandchildren join the flow, streaming into Bangalore in search of work as labourers or security guards. They throng the steps of Kuppam station, crowding the train well before it has even clanged to a halt. Only the old folk are left in the fields, looking up at the fierce, empty sky. 🐦

Ogo Sh

ANINDYA ROY

ANINDYA ROY is a writer and illustrator of graphic novels. He co-founded the graphic-novel publisher Phantomville and is founder and director of the Delhi Comic Arts Festival (DeCAF). His work has been supported by the British Council, the Alliance Française, Pro Helvetia, the Indian Foundation for the Arts and the National Foundation for India. He is currently working on a travel series in the graphic-novel format.

uncho!

Writer and illustrator Anindya Roy shines a light on Bengali food culture through the lens of his Kolkata family, who have been 'expatriates' in New Delhi since 1946. With illustrations by the author.

Ogo Shuncho! 'Hello! Listen!' is a Bengali term of endearment often used in place of given names between husband and wife.

79

Fish

In Delhi back in the 1970s we were not exposed to a wide range of cuisines; the key daily driver of our household was Bengali food. This was not something forced upon us; it was declared theatrically many times during the course of the day, in poems, stories and monologues, that Bengali food was the best in the world.

BENGALI FOOD IS THE BEST IN THE WORLD.

DON'T GET ME STARTED ON WESTERN FOOD. IT'S JUST MEAT, POTATOES, BREAD, BUTTER, CHEESE. BLAND!

This was not supported through having experienced 'the food of the others', however. The people who made such claims had never sampled non-Bengali cuisine such as a pizza or a burger or something south Indian or Japanese – never! – or maybe once, but that was enough to declare all non-Bengali food unfit for Bengali consumption. Some gentrified version of an otherwise rich and robust north-Indian dish might occasionally make it to the table in the form of a chickpea, red-kidney-bean or paneer curry, but this would cause mild-to-moderate levels of trepidation.

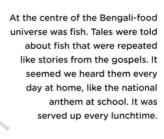

At the centre of the Bengali-food universe was fish. Tales were told about fish that were repeated like stories from the gospels. It seemed we heard them every day at home, like the national anthem at school. It was served up every lunchtime.

Fish could not be faulted – unless, of course, it was saltwater fish (one was allowed to offer mild criticism of fish from the sea). Freshwater fish, however, was the tastiest, most divine food you could put in your mouth when served in a Bengali fashion. Besides being the tastiest damn thing on the planet it was also unbelievably beneficial to health.

WHAT BREED OF BENGALI DOESN'T LIKE FISH?

It had the combined qualities of Superman, broccoli, berries, Batman, aloe vera, Wonder Woman, green tea, every Nobel laureate, Garry Kasparov, kale, Gandhi, spirulina, Mandela and whatever and whoever else might come to mind.

If you were someone who might find fault with fish or any of the many Bengali fish recipes – such as machar jhal (a carp curry) or ilish with mustard seeds or prawns with gourd or any of the other numerous preparations – those around you would try to cure you as if you had an illness or a tumour. Two of my issues with fish were the fiddly bones and its stench. What I referred to as 'stench' was called 'aroma' by the rest of my twenty-odd family members. Given my lack of enthusiasm for and scepticism towards Bengali fish dishes, I was considered something of a black sheep in need of steering in the right direction, so I had to endure the endless wisdoms imparted by the rest of the family on matters pertaining to fish.

THE BENGALI MATRIX

Digestion and exercise

Digesting food was another daily foray into nothingness. Discomfort in the form of 'acidity' showed its ugly face after every meal. But why? they all wondered helplessly. Whenever they suffered from indigestion they would list the tasks they had performed that day and which, according to them, were so tedious and demanding that it should have accelerated their metabolism instead of giving them heartburn: 'I had to walk so far in the office to get tea because the help was on leave.'

WHAT? I WAS TOLD TO WARM UP BEFORE I GOT STARTED.

'I cleaned out my whole *almirah*, which meant I even had to lift my heavy wedding saris.' 'I took a bath in four buckets of water, which required me to carry four buckets of water from the tap in the courtyard to the bathroom.' (Distance: four metres.) 'I washed the vegetables, chopped them and then cooked the whole pilau.'

They would list these daily chores in rotation, adding minute details and dramas along the way. As a result, even the simple act of tying a shoelace would sound as if someone had scaled Everest and then run all the way home. What they meant was, this was quite enough exercise. That anything more than this might give them an ugly body packed with huge, rippling muscles like Arnold Schwarzenegger, or age their limbs, bones and organs faster by putting them under unnecessary strain.

I'LL BE BACK ...

... FOR THE BAKED RASGULLA FROM KAMALA SWEETS.

Afterwards they would all gather round with the many Ayurvedic, homoeopathic and other pharmaceutical products that they had neatly tucked away in their well-organised individual medicine chests and further debate about what they should be consuming today to tackle the problem at hand before discussing the menu for tomorrow.

SUICIDE SQUAT

LUCHI

(DEEP-FRIED FLAT BREAD)

KOSHA
MANGSHO

(RICH MUTTON CURRY)

It never occurred to any one of them that they might benefit from exercising a bit more or eating a few raw vegetables once in a while or tweaking the diet a bit or eating less or maybe not consuming something fried at every meal. Instead, there was bewilderment and disappointment, as if the government, the United Nations and the Delhi Police had all let them down again.

The few activities I do recall being carried out solely as exercise were: a gentle stroll of about twenty to thirty paces along the balcony while restlessly waiting for snack vendors; randomly wiggling the digits of the feet while lying in a horizontal position and stating that this act was 'extremely beneficial' for the whole nervous system; occasionally rolling and stretching the arms after slapping the TV around to achieve a better satellite signal; stretching the legs on the sofa in the manner recommended to passengers on long-haul flights; trying to reach an itch on their backs, where one saw their hands twist and turn giving the illusion that they were attempting some challenging yoga pose.

Chakrasana

YOGA

Eating out

During their schooldays in Delhi, my uncles and aunts could only just about afford to eat street food; eating out at a decent restaurant with air conditioning was the height of luxury to which very few could stretch. One of the clear street favourites was chaat in its many forms.

ONE MORE?

NO! CAN'T YOU SEE I'M WATCHING MY FIGURE? 24 WILL BE PLENTY.

OMG, THE ALOO TIKKI LOOKS AMAZING. I WISH TODAY WAS CHEAT DAY ...

Just like Marvel has a universe of superheroes, chaat is a universe of dishes with a 'snack-like' orientation. One of them is golgappa (called puchka in Bengal), which is a fried hollow crispy ball of wheat flour or semolina, roughly four centimetres in diameter, filled with cold spiced tamarind water, chutney, chickpeas, potatoes and tangy masala. It fits snugly in the palm of one's hand, and it's not hard to put away six to ten of these at a time.

Peanuts were a clear favourite because of their 'carry me anywhere, eat me any time' attitude. You could rummage through anyone's pocket or handbag and find some (the unshelled variety), particularly during winter. On Sundays there were huge gossip sessions around mounds of peanuts piled up on a folding camp-bed in the courtyard. While the nuts were being consumed the conversation never strayed far from how much they missed the street food of Kolkata, the kathi rolls, the ghugni, the jhalmuri, the telebhajas, the kabiraji cutlet, the Mughlai paratha, etc., a list that seemed never-ending.

ONE MUTTON KATHI ...

Weddings were another opportunity to eat out. Inviting our extended family to a wedding meant dealing with fifty or sixty hungry souls. We were always something of a mob at such events. Our first victims would be the waiters serving non-vegetarian snacks; we attacked those snacks in the same way that the migrating wagons were attacked by Native Americans in western movies. Our appetite was huge compared with the limited serving capacity of the waiters' trays, so it took many trips on their part to satisfy us before moving on to the other guests. At times they had to hide from us or change their route just to be able to get past.

The wisest of the elders would look at your plate with disgust if it was bereft of something non-vegetarian at any point during the wedding buffet. If you were seen with some salad vegetables or a lentil curry you would be mocked for months. A mountain of non-vegetarian delights should fill your plate and, when finished, a heap of bones such as that found in a carnivore's cave should be all that remained.

DR A: I CAN'T DECIDE HOW MANY VOLTS TO GIVE HIM.

DR B: WHAT'S HIS PROBLEM?

DR A: HE'S BEEN EATING THE VEGETARIAN FOOD AT WEDDINGS.

DR B: OMG! GIVE HIM THE MAX!

Nowadays alcohol seems to have become common at weddings, but back then it was rare to see liquor at Bengali nuptials. From not being served at all, the time came when it would be found stashed in the back of somebody's car. Male guests would be sent clandestine messages throughout the wedding party by other menfolk already in the know, advising them to come to this mysterious vehicle with the promise that their mood would be elevated. It seemed to me then that alcohol was always drunk furtively, as if there were something guilt inducing, sinful and illegal associated with its consumption. During family parties you rarely spotted anyone actually drinking, but the smell of alcohol was very much present. Men of eligible drinking age were found aiming for dark corners like cold-war spies, or they would vanish for longish periods of time only to return with a partly guilty, partly jovial expression on their faces. The drink of choice for most seemed to be rum – it was cheap – and Old Monk was a clear hit with poor and rich alike. Beer was cumbersome to store and good whisky was expensive.

Bengali Sweets

I think one of the principal reasons that back pain was prevalent in my household was because most of the older generation spent a great deal of time bent over looking into the fridge and rooting around inside searching for something. They were persistent.

Only now that I have started to do the same thing at least three times a day do I realise what this intense activity was all about: they were combing the fridge for sweets more diligently than suspect nations are searched for weapons of mass destruction. It was assumed that there would always be some leftover sweet item that everyone else would have forgotten about and which could be excavated from the bowels of the refrigerator – and the truth of the matter is that one did find a dry sweet like a sandesh or a kanchagolla almost every time, even in a house with twenty people and only one fridge.

The casual way in which sweets were consumed even by the resident diabetics was alarming. Most justified the intake of something sweet with escapist philosophies and by passing off highly questionable statements as medical facts in favour of this behaviour. A couple of days without sweets troubled every soul. Some complained of nightmares, disorientation, memory loss, lack of physical flexibility and of losing the will to live and suchlike. One uncle used to sleep with a bowl full of sweets next to his bedside; upon being challenged about this he said that it made him feel less anxious when returning from his bathroom breaks. When relatives turned up from Kolkata they would bring suitcases full of confectionary. Some argued that with the right kind of advertising and exposure, Bengali sweet-making could achieve a similar status to that of Swiss cheese-making. Our relatives still call us regularly to give updates on what new experimental sweets are being created in Kolkata.

The thing that I admire the most about Bengali food culture is the passion that surrounds it. Since childhood I heard those in the house describe food in the most imaginative ways. However it started out, every conversation soon turned to the subject of food, and the transition was not forced; it felt very natural. One would hear statements like: 'The fish was so fresh that I felt like someone just threw me in a tub of icy water.' 'The rice was so fragrant and aromatic that people called from as far as D Block three kilometres away to enquire about it and congratulate me.' Then there were the ghost stories associated with food. One uncle told us: 'At the two-storeyed Baranagar house in Kolkata in 1943 late one evening, some of us cousins sat in the living room and thought, "How wonderful it would be to have luchi [a kind of deep-fried flat bread] and kumro'r chokka [pumpkin curry]," and lo!, a rumbling noise came from the roof, and a large pumpkin tumbled down the stairs.'

DID SOMEONE JUST THINK ABOUT A DAAB CHINGRI? (PRAWNS IN GREEN COCONUT)

IF YOU COME ANY FURTHER INTO THE HOUSE WITH THAT VEGETABLE ALL BONDS OF BLOOD WILL BE BROKEN.

Our parents tried to instil the value of trying every kind of food that appeared on our plates. This training worked for most of my cousins, but unfortunately I remain staunchly opposed to the gourd family, whether bottle, round, plain or snake gourd. If I find one on my plate or spot one anywhere nearby, I feel like a Spartan warrior who must defend his honour.

Older relatives would stand behind you and pester you about how one should eat, what should be eaten first, into which dish you should squeeze a bit of lemon or crush a bit of green chilli. Seeing an uncle stick a whole bata – one of the boniest fish around – in his mouth and then extract the whole skeleton intact seemed like a magic trick. I came to the conclusion a while back that, while there are a few dishes that I can possibly do without, the passionate discourse around Bengali food is absolutely indispensable to me.

THE ONE AND ONLY RULE FOR EATING FISH CURRY: CRUSH THE CHILLI INTO THE RICE LIKE YOU'RE TEACHING IT A LESSON FOR INSULTING YOUR MOTHER.

Holding Back the Night: Secularism Under Siege

JULIA LAUTER

Translated by Jana Marlene Mader

A man washes in the Ganges
at dawn in Varanasi.

In the land of spirituality, gurus and holy men – and where Hindu nationalism rules the roost – there seems to be no place for non-believers, a minority abhorred by all religions as they attempt to pursue their rationalist struggle in the face of murder and intimidation.

89

DISENCHANTMENT

Darkness doesn't fall all at once. It slips unnoticed into our midst; drop by drop it feeds the twilight until suddenly all is black night.

In India the onset of darkness began with a weeping crucifix. On 10 March 2012 hundreds of pilgrims crowd into a small alleyway in Vile Parle, a sleepy neighbourhood in the north-west of the twenty-million metropolis that is Mumbai. They are crouching close to the floor; it is stuffy, narrow and dusty. A two-metre-high wooden cross is prominent in their midst, a Messiah figure affixed to it. Drops of water run from the feet of the Son of God, and these are collected by priests and passed to the faithful. The pilgrims wet their foreheads and their lips; drinking the tears of the cross, so the priests promise, will bring them happiness and good health. People kneel in the dust and pray to the weeping cross.

Sanal Edamaruku makes his way through the crowd. He is, as always, impeccably dressed, his goatee neatly trimmed. The middle-aged man wears a blossom-white shirt and walks up to the cross with the self-assured elegance of a trained classical Indian dancer. Edamaruku is president of the Indian Rationalist Association, a renowned guru-buster, notorious for debunking the claims to mystical powers of gurus and magicians. He is here at the invitation of representatives of the Catholic Church after denying on a talk show that miracles really do take place on this earth.

He has travelled all the way from Delhi, a thousand kilometres away, to rob the pilgrims of their miracle.

Under the suspicious glare of the faithful, he examines the base of the cross, the adjacent wall, the ground surrounding it. Edamaruku is wary. In Mumbai, the multi-ethnic, multi-faith mega-city, the scars of religious riots are a reminder of how thin that line is that separates divine ecstasy and bloody fanaticism.

Edamaruku spots algae on a nearby wall and follows its trail. Behind a hut, only a few metres from the cross, lies the explanation for the miracle of Vile Parle: the weeping wooden cross is the dripping end of a blocked waste pipe. As a result of capillary action in the wood, the stinking broth has been sucked upwards and drips from the hole made by the nail attaching the wooden Saviour to the crucifix. Pure physics. 'Hundreds of pilgrims have rubbed themselves with sewage all this time,' says Edamaruku today, still shaking his head in disbelief.

To confirm his hypothesis he takes a water sample and leaves the pilgrimage site as quickly as possible. 'For the truth, they would have torn me to pieces on the spot,' he says today. Edamaruku – who grew up in an atheist household; who, according to his own account, was the first pupil in India to win the right in a court of law to sign up for school without having to state caste or religion; who toured India as a student in an old van to spread secularism – knows where his rhetorical skills

JULIA LAUTER is a reporter and writer who works for a number of high-profile magazines in Germany and internationally, including *Reportagen*, *Süddeutsche Zeitung Magazin*, the weekend *Tageszeitung* and *Amnesty Journal*. Over the last decade she has travelled extensively throughout India with longer stays for study and research. In 2018 she developed an interest in the south-Indian anti-religious social reformer Periyar, becoming passionate about the history of the Indian rationalist movement. She works with a number of theatres and curates exhibitions of literary documentation.

Above: Bathers at dawn in Varanasi.

work best. This same evening he wants to debunk the miracle in a discussion on the regional channel TV9. The television appearance is to cast a shadow over his life. A shadow under which he will remain.

Some are of the opinion that Sanal Edamaruku has only himself to blame; that he came over as vain; that his aim was not to convince but to shine. He himself conjured up the curse of the weeping cross that night.

Think of India, and religion will come to mind. No street without a temple, no house without icons, gurus or babas. On the bumper of almost every car hangs a string of chillies, limes and coal to protect against accidents. This is a harmless superstition, but what if people don't go to the doctor because healers tell them the illness is an evil spirit? What if the mere suspicion that you might be in possession of some beef mobilises murderous lynch mobs? What if the Ministry of Health advises better bodily hygiene and yoga as a treatment for depression? What if, as happened in October 2018, disputes are settled in the highest state investigative authority in the presence of a spiritual teacher?

Cracks quickly start to appear in the image of India as a spiritual fairyland once you take a closer look. The simplification of Indian culture is a dangerous distortion, Nobel laureate Amartya Sen warned in an interview in 2006, not only outside

the country but also within Indian society itself. The Hindu-nationalist BJP has ruled the country since 2014, and many of the party's supporters want a pure Hindu nation. Although the party leadership is more moderate in its public pronouncements, there is much for religious minorities – Muslims, Christians, Jains and Parsees – to worry about, and this is even more true for those who speak out against any belief in miracles: the rationalists.

In the 2011 census some three million people in India said they did not belong to any religion, a threefold increase on the previous survey ten years earlier and a bigger increase than that found in any of the country's religious communities. At the same time, pressure is growing on them: in September 2017 journalist Gauri Lankesh was shot in front of her house, the latest in a series of murders of prominent rationalists that had already taken the lives of a literary scholar, a politician and a doctor, Narendra Dabholkar.

What unites the murder victims is that they were all engaged in the fight against superstition and for a pluralistic society. In the febrile atmosphere of a country infected with the viral belief of cultural and religious purity, where religious conflicts are used as a path to power and the most radical adherents to all religions have become thin skinned, many regard this agenda as a declaration of war. Gauri Lankesh wrote in a private email exchange with her ex-husband shortly before her assassination: 'I have had enough of fighting against the fascist forces. I have had enough of banging my head against the wall ... The world is becoming insufferable to live in.' Three months after Lankesh was shot a BJP minister of state declared that

THE FIRST ATHEISTS

Atheism and criticism of religion are often seen as a consequence of Enlightenment thinking in Europe. As early as 600 BCE, however, the Charvaka school in India believed neither in deities nor life after death and rejected religious rites. Some students of religious history believe that followers of this philosophy were the world's first atheists, long before Europe was shaken by Enlightenment ideas of a life without faith. But traces of this tradition were lost in the 16th century. The rationalist movements of contemporary India have their roots in the reform movement of the 19th century and were, in fact, strongly influenced by European atheism through writings that were widely circulated in colonial India. In those days atheists were mainly known as free thinkers. In the early 20th century rationalism became a widespread concept, both as a school of thought and to label those whom believers describe as having 'strayed from the faith'.

the word 'secular' should be removed from the constitution. The enemies of rationalism were getting themselves into position.

It was around this time, according to the rationalists, that the mood in India shifted and all-out war was declared on the non-believers. This is the story of three generations of rationalists who are in the firing line today, each generation in its own way. There is the rhetorician Sanal Edamaruku, who for decades fought intellectual battles in the name of religious criticism; there is the mediator Hamid Dabholkar, who lost his father in the fight for reason in India and now continues in his Enlightenment-driven tradition; and there is the activist Chaitali Shinde, who today plots the resistance online and at clandestine meetings. Their common history is that of the struggle for reason and freedom of opinion in India – and it has only just begun.

Back in early 2012, when the weeping crucifix still hung in Vile Parle, Sanal Edamaruku was still the spokesman for the enlightened rhetoricians and his life had not yet been shattered by the new radicalism. On the evening following his visit to the weeping cross he sits in a studio, eloquently engaging in an argument with representatives of the Catholic Church. His trump card is the water analysis. It has confirmed his hypothesis. Not a divine miracle but a blocked drain has caused the cross weep. Edamaruku accuses the Church of exploiting people's ignorance and using supposed miracles to improve its finances.

The Church delegates – among them a priest, a lawyer and a representative of the Catholic community – are beside themselves with rage. The bishop of Mumbai, Agnelo Rufino Gracias, is brought in to say that the Church has not marketed the cross as a miracle and that it has a long tradition of promoting science. 'On my side are discoverers like Galileo Galilei and humanists like Leonardo Bruni,' Sanal Edamaruku replies. 'On your side, Pope Benedict, who advocates exorcism.' The dispute escalates, and the bishop demands an apology. When Edamaruku refuses, the bishop, to camera, makes an ominous pronouncement: with his comments the gurubuster has insulted the Church and must be brought to justice. End of discussion. When, shortly afterwards, Edamaruku tries to leave the studio he is stopped by employees of the broadcaster. Outside the studio an angry crowd is waiting for him. 'I was scared to death for the first time,' says Edamaruku. 'They came with sticks, and they came to kill me.' He has to hold out in the studio for several hours before he can escape through the back exit in the early hours of the morning.

The next day the newspapers report that the bishop will press blasphemy charges against Edamaruku. Section 295a of the Indian Penal Code is a relic of British rule. It came into force in 1927 and it states that anyone who offends the religious feelings of any group can be punished by up to three years in prison. Edamaruku says that by explaining the supposed miracle he was only doing his civic duty, because the Indian Constitution says that all citizens of India should 'develop the scientific temper, humanism and the spirit of inquiry and reform'. Back in Delhi he prepares to take the dispute to court. 'I already had lawyers who wanted to represent me *pro bono*. My case was a great opportunity to bury Section 295a and strengthen freedom of speech.'

But even before the Church representatives can bring the charges, Edamaruku gets a call from the intelligence service of the Ministry of the Interior to inform him that certain militant groups are calling for his death rather than a trial. Facebook groups are eagerly discussing how to 'ritually clean him with pain'. Edamaruku receives police protection. He moves into a friend's house, then into a room on the campus of the university in Delhi. He hides there for a month and a half. A dark time. Edamaruku feels torn from his life. At the beginning of July his hiding place is discovered and he is placed under surveillance. Edamaruku sends a call for help to the wider network of atheists. The president of the Finnish Humanist Association, Pekka Elo, who works at the Ministry of Education in Finland, answers promptly: he should apply for a visa at the Finnish embassy by noon. Edamaruku goes to the embassy in a taxi. 'I didn't have anything with me: no ticket, no clothes, only 210 euros in cash.' He gets a visa, and his contact arranges for a ticket to be given to him for a Finnair flight the following morning. 'Only when the aircraft began to roll, the burden fell off me. I sent a message to some close friends that I was safe now.' Then he turns off his phone and falls asleep. Behind him he leaves the social twilight of India; before him, just seven hours away, is the Finnish summer, where it never gets dark.

Edamaruku thought at that time that he would only be in exile for a few months, but he is still there, and there is no end in sight. From his apartment in Helsinki he worked for a long time as an editor of the atheistic polemical publications *Modern Freethinker* and *Therali*. Today he writes books and articles and attends international conferences. He still runs the Indian Rationalist Association. Almost every evening he sits in front of his computer to keep in touch with his comrades. His movement remains strong, he says, with 120,000 members in more than 225 local groups.

You can reach Edamaruku in his Finnish exile via Skype. The president of the rationalists speaks calmly, always anxious to highlight the positive side to his story. The long Finnish winter, he says, makes things difficult at times. 'You can walk or drive for hours without meeting anyone – I like the silence and the peace,' he explains during a video call. On many evenings only the blue glow of the screen illuminates Edamaruku's apartment. 'I have spent most of my life in the hustle and bustle of Delhi. This is a stark contrast.'

Once, in August 2013, he was close to leaving his exile. His friend Narendra Dabholkar, an influential leading thinker of the movement, tried to persuade him to return. 'He said my escape would demoralise the rationalists in India. He said his movement was now big enough to provide my security. Come back, he said.' Sanal Edamaruku pauses, breathing heavily. 'Four days after that conversation he was dead.' On 20 August 2013, at 7.20 a.m., Narendra Dabholkar was shot in the street.

And all at once the darkest night covered the world of Indian rationalism.

DISILLUSIONMENT

Until that fateful morning in 2013 Narendra Dabholkar's habit is to go for a walk every Monday and Tuesday before the heat of the day crushes the city. He appreciates the view from the Shinde Bridge in the centre of Pune: how the rising sun is reflected from the east in the river Mula, how it surrounds the mighty water buffaloes that graze in the meadows and how it makes the magnificent Omkareshwar Mandir temple on the bank opposite shine a bright pink. Dabholkar is a man of routine who never goes without his walk – despite the death threats. 'If I have to take police protection in my own country from my own people, then there is something wrong with me,' he said once in an interview. 'I'm fighting within the framework of the Indian

Can one of India's most influential entrepreneurs really be a yoga guru who has renounced all material possessions? Just turn on the TV or take a look at the billboards that line the roads, and there he is, Baba Ramdev, in his orange robes and wooden sandals, demonstrating his yoga poses while advertising the Ayurvedic products sold by his company Patanjali. Born into a peasant family, the young Ramdev embarked on a career as a yoga teacher in the 1990s and set out in search of herbs to produce his famous medicines with Acharya Balkrishna – today the company's managing director and one of the world's richest men. It was during those years that Ramdev renounced earthly goods to live as an ascetic, or *sanyasi*. But he was driven by a mission to safeguard India's well-being and prestige by restoring the art of yoga and Indian medical traditions to their ancient glory, so in the early 2000s he started presenting a TV programme and founded Patanjali. As a result, not just medicines but turmeric toothpaste, saffron soap and detergents made from cows' urine have found their way into Indian households: a patriotic choice, in line with the nationalism of Modi's BJP. Baba Ramdev is now a star. A star in sandals costing 400 rupees (around $3). Because the guru who founded India's fastest-growing company is technically not its owner, nor does he receive a salary: how could he when he has taken a vow of poverty?

Constitution, and it is not against anyone but for everyone.'

On this August morning witnesses claim to see two people on a motorcycle racing up behind a man as he walks along. Four shots follow – two hitting Dabholkar, one in the back of the head, one in his back – and the perpetrators race off towards the city. Narendra Dabholkar dies on the bridge with a view of the flowing river, the pink temple, while the sky fills with startled black kites.

Perhaps he should have been more careful, says his son. Hamid Dabholkar takes off his glasses, puts his hands in front of his eyes. After a short pause he puts them back on carefully and continues speaking softly. 'But none of us believed that something like this could really happen.' The forty-year-old psychiatrist sits in a small, sparsely furnished second-floor office in a dark backyard. He runs a rehab clinic here in the sleepy town of Satara, Maharashtra. Nobody on the street knows the name of the foundation that finances this institution – but anyone who asks for Dabholkar is immediately given directions.

Hamid Dabholkar looks very young. His black hair falls deep over his forehead; his face is closed; his thick moustache is like a badge of adulthood, an attempt at gravitas. The murder of his father, Narendra Dabholkar, not only robbed him of his life but also destroyed his life's work. Now the son is trying to put the pieces back together one at a time.

What did his father do to become the target of such an attack? In the late 1980s Narendra Dabholkar worked as a doctor in his home town of Satara. Being raised in a rationalist family, he had for years been active in the fight against the caste system, supporting people who studied, worked and married regardless of caste boundaries. But he was no match for the elders

THE PASSENGER   Julia Lauter

in the villages and towns, those who pre-served the old traditions and who, to this day, continue to hand out severe punish-ments to those who defy tradition, while reformers are systematically defamed and sabotaged. Because he believed he could inspire more people to change, Dabholkar turned his attention to superstition and formed the Committee for Eradication of Blind Faith in Maharashtra: MANS (Maharashtra Andhashraddha Nirmoolan Samiti). 'I don't believe in God or religion. But the people around me believe in God and religion. And I don't think I can achieve anything without connecting with them.' These words of the philosopher and poet Narhar Ambadas Kurundkar inspired Dabholkar. To join MANS one did not have to be an atheist; one should simply be pre-pared to question oneself and one's faith critically. The rest would follow, Dabholkar believed.

The movement grew quickly. Many thousands of volunteers taught students and teachers the art of critical debate. In a country where to enquire is considered disrespectful, where to believe is more applauded than to understand, Dabholkar and his fellow campaigners aimed to create a new generation of critical spirits. The movement made a lot of enemies – par-ticularly with a proposal by Dabholkar and others in 2003 for a law that would outlaw black magic. The law was aimed at prac-tices that exploit superstitious belief such as human sacrifice, exorcism and fraudu-lent claims of possessing healing powers. The radical powers in the country accused Dabholkar of being anti-religious and anti-Hindu, and the threats intensified.

'My father fought for this law for years,' says his son Hamid Dabholkar. 'He put all his hopes in it, that this would push back the darkness in the country.' Hamid Dabholkar nervously fiddles with his pen. 'Sadly, the law was not passed till six days after my father's murder and came into effect three months later.' The pen starts to rotate more quickly.

Around five hundred cases have since been processed under the Anti-Superstition and Black Magic Act. Today MANS has five thousand members, more than ever. 'The seed of rationalism cannot be killed with weapons. My father knew that,' he says. Since the murder, the son has been under police protection around the clock, as have his sister and mother. In front of the door of his office sits an inconspicuous man in a black suit, part of a special police unit. 'I'm afraid. We're all afraid ...' Dabholkar adds, and, after a moment's pause. 'This is a natural reaction.'

He seems torn between his roles as mourning son and analysing psychiatrist. 'Since his murder I am not myself any more,' he says. 'I live my father's dream – even if I know that this is an unsolved, complicated processing of pain.' It is his decision and his way, he adds almost defi-antly, and he appears even younger than before.

Growing up in a secular family, Hamid and his sister Mukta were removed from the rites and customs that shaped life around them. He first became aware that his family was different at nine years of age when his fourth-grade class was taught the story of the battle of the Hindu command-ers against the Muslim Mughal emperors, and other children began to tease him about his Muslim first name, given to him in honour of the Muslim social reformer

'"We're not interested in intellectual know-it-alls; our rationalism is supposed to really help people."'

Hamid Dalwai. When, after school, he complained to his father about the teasing the only response he got was, 'Names have no religion.'

Hamid Dabholkar says the answer satisfied him. Religion, that was for other people. Hamid and Mukta grew up as part of the movement – but it was only after the murder of their father that they were catapulted from the periphery into the centre. 'We're not interested in intellectual know-it-alls; our rationalism is supposed to really help people,' the psychiatrist says. This is what underpins his day clinic, which he runs alongside the rehab clinic at his parents' house. Pictures of his ancestors hang on the clay walls – but his father has not yet found a place in their ranks. 'When he was still here he was always on the road; I hardly saw him,' says Hamid Dabholkar. Today he sees him every day, here or in the clinic, in the movement as a whole. 'He is always there now.'

The MANS movement chose the Shinde Bridge as a symbol of its determination: since the murder of 'the Doctor', as his followers affectionately refer to him, they have organised a demonstration there on the 20th of every month. 'We go to where he lost his life to keep up the public pressure on the investigations,' says his son. The case of his father's murder has not yet been solved. For years Narendra Dabholkar was the victim of accusations and threats from radical Hindu circles, notably from Sanatan Sanstha (SS), a Hindu organisation from Goa whose stated goal is to unify Hindu spirituality and knowledge, although experts describe it as a kind of Scientology for orthodox Hindus. The cult, founded in 1999 by a hypnotherapist, has made headlines since 2007 for its connection to bomb attacks. SS members take part in combat training with the weapon of the god Shiva, the trident. In its numerous publications the group invokes a third world war and makes the claim that a bullet shot to the accompaniment of prayers will never miss its target. At their annual conferences lists are issued of those who oppose its causes: Narendra Dabholkar was at the top of that list for years.

Five years after he was shot down on the Shinde Bridge the federal police declared the murder of Narendra Dabholkar to be a terrorist act, confirming the view that the rationalist was murdered with the deliberate aim of spreading unrest and terror. Although this was a source of satisfaction for the family, hardly anyone within the movement believes that justice will be done. 'All political camps have failed to fight radical elements with a strong hand,' says Hamid Dabholkar. When talk turns to politics he speaks even more quietly, weighing up every word. He scrutinises his interviewer, looks over at the policeman there to protect him sitting a few metres away. After everything that has happened

Left: A child is blessed at his first-birthday celebration in New Delhi.

it is hard for him to trust anyone. Almost whispering, he adds, 'If our democracy were to work, my father would still be alive.'

Every day Hamid Dabholkar reads the comments under the articles about his father's murder. 'There are thousands who approve of this act, thousands whose minds are full of hatred.' Sometimes, he says, despair rises in him. The struggle against darkness can last a lifetime; it can even cost you your life. But whether the struggle will ever bring light, no one can say.

REBELLION

And suddenly, in the blink of an eye, the darkness becomes tangible. An old woman stands in a living room and convulses while divinely possessed. Her body squirms under the delicate fabric of her green sari. In the middle of her forehead there is a big red dot, the *bindi*. The woman opens her eyes. Suddenly laughter roars from her chest, then a howl, a moan and a groan. With a quick movement she loosens her knotted hair, and the grey strands fall over her face. She moves through the room, arms and legs flailing. In one hand she holds a white fingernail-sized block of camphor. She lights it, puts the flame close to her face and places it on her tongue. The fire blazes as she slowly closes her mouth. She pauses for a moment, then spits it out. Vandana Shinde looks up, her gaze suddenly clear, her voice calm. 'It's all tricks,' she says calmly. Then the 72-year-old puts her hair back into an elegant bun and falls into a deep armchair.

Magic is very big business in India, with thousands of self-proclaimed magicians claiming to be able to swallow swords or fire, lie on beds of nails or bend iron. In lucrative roadshows that make a spectacle out of superstition, the tricksters promise their bewildered and ignorant spectators

COW VIGILANTES

'Stray' cows that have been set free after growing too old to be productive are a common sight in India. Hindus account for 80 per cent of India's population, and the protection of these animals, which they regard as sacred, is a subject close to many people's hearts: there are laws to protect them, and slaughtering cattle is illegal in almost every state. In recent years, however, groups known as cow vigilantes have decided to take enforcement of the law into their own hands. These militias are made up of young men with little education recruited by nationalist groups. They patrol the countryside at night, armed, in search of vehicles transporting cows. Sometimes they merely pass on their suspicions to the police but are increasingly taking it upon themselves to dispense justice. Those affected are almost exclusively minorities: most of the victims are Muslims, Dalits or Adivasi. In September 2015 Mohammad Akhlaq, a 56-year-old Muslim, was dragged out of his house, hit on the head with a brick and killed – all because of a rumour that he had beef in his house. This was no isolated incident: violence linked to cows resulted in hundreds of attacks between 2012 and 2018. Between 2015 and 2018, at least forty-four people, thirty-six of them Muslim, were killed in twelve Indian states. There has been a steep rise in these violent episodes since 2014 when the BJP came to power. Protecting cows was a recurring theme in the electoral campaign fought by Modi and his party, who have never distanced themselves from these punitive raids.

Above: A procession in honour
of the guru Ravidas in New Delhi.

that they are able to heal all kinds of conditions – from cancer and schizophrenia to poverty and heartache – in return for money. Vandana Shinde fights against this. The retired administrator has been touring Maharashtra on her own for twenty years. Her performances have a different finale from those of the tricksters, however, since at the end of her show she explains how her tricks are done. Vandana Shinde sows doubt among the superstitious – without being paid, of course. Who would pay for the debunking of miracles?

During the performance her daughter stands still in the background, arms folded. 'I couldn't do that, these performances in front of hundreds of people,' says Chaitali Shinde. The 42-year-old looks like her mother – petite and dainty and dressed traditionally. She wears a salwar kameez, a dark-green shirt dress with matching trousers and shawl. But you don't have to spend long in her company to realise that in attitude, if not in dress, she is far from traditional. 'I believe people pray to reach a state of zombie-like deafness. But I always wanted clarity and reason in my life,' she says.

In her apartment Shinde speaks freely about her lack of belief. Since her parents were already sceptics, rationalism has always played a role in her life, she says. Yet outside her home she chooses her words cautiously: she, too, has been marked by

the attacks on those who think the way she does. It has taken a long time for this single mother to make peace with her sense of being different. Away from her family she has always kept her lack of belief hidden, as a child at school, as a teenager at university, even today at work (where she develops digital training services for companies). Being an atheist is a taboo in many areas of Indian life. People without faith are regarded as dry and joyless – at worst, lacking in culture and morality.

Her rationalism was also behind the failure of her marriage to a traditional Hindu, she says. 'I wanted to analyse our problems in the relationship; my ex-husband said we would argue over a wrongly hung mirror and the resulting spatial energy.' The unanimous view of the couple's friends is that Chaitali Shinde's lack of faith was to blame for the break-up. Today she lives with her mother, her brother and her daughter in an avowedly rationalist household. 'When we argue, at least we don't blame the furniture for it,' she says.

But how much can one close oneself off from the outside world? How long can one defy the darkness? Among the many Indians who eat beef at home, drink alcohol and do not practise any religion there is a fear that religious extremism increasingly has ex-Hindus, ex-Muslims and ex-Christians in its sights. In a country where a lynch mob can be mobilised by rumour alone, the sense of an existential threat to those who think differently is not new. What if the kids talk at school? What if marginalisation turns into open violence? Chaitali

Shinde long had the sense that she should do something about the situation herself, but she did not act until after Narendra Dabholkar was murdered. The famous rationalist had been a friend of her parents. The day after his assassination Chaitali Shinde spoke to hundreds of people in the street in front of the district administrative offices in her home town, Thane, on the north-eastern outskirts of Mumbai. She was shocked by the news, sought company and conversation because she did not want to feel alone in her bewilderment. There was widespread agreement that the murder had been intended to consolidate the right-wing extremist forces in the country. Further attacks on freedom of thought and speech were to be expected. And so the rationalists decided to hit back. With reason and the power of community as their weapons.

They formed a group they called We the Brights. As a light in the darkness. Many old-school rationalists – Hamid Dabholkar among them – criticised the name, saying the note of arrogance would send the wrong signals out and lead to further polarisation rather than understanding. But the newly energised rationalists have stuck with it, intending it to be a signpost into a future where non-believers no longer have to apologise. 'We have lost faith that the small battles against superstition and miracle healers can dispel darkness in this country,' says Chaitali Shinde.

Since its formation in 2013 We the Brights has rapidly grown to a membership of more than four thousand, and they meet online as well as in person. 'On the internet we are a closed group, where we can simply let out all the frustration. Over the fact that everyone thinks we're crazy. That everyone around us seeks their salvation at statues and crosses. That sometimes you'd just like to torch all that shit ...' Chaitali Shinde adds

'As people squeeze through the alleyways they stop at their respective god, touch the feet of the statue or the cross and hurry on. Children, old people, women in saris, men with tribal tattoos. Many don't even allow their act of worship to interrupt their phone call.'

quickly, 'even if we would never do that, of course.' Sometimes it's enough to know that there are a few like-minded people out there.

Outside the virtual safe spaces, the Brights meet in secret. To get to their meeting point you must be guided through a series of alleys, each smaller than the last, of the fishing village on the Worli peninsula. Long before there was a metropolis here, when it was seven sleepy islands poking out of the mangrove swamps, the Koli people lived on this headland that juts out into the Arabian Sea in western Mumbai.

In the last hundred metres before the meeting place there are three temples, one church, one mosque and countless statues and small shrines. As people squeeze through the alleyways they stop at their respective god, touch the feet of the statue or the cross and hurry on. Children, old people, women in saris, men with tribal tattoos. Many don't even allow their act of worship to interrupt their phone call.

The house of today's host is painted bright orange. He states proudly that he built it himself. In the old way of thinking he belongs to the casteless, the Dalits; in the world of rationalists there are to be no castes, no distinctions. 'It's good to have normal people around,' says Chaitali Shinde. Surrounded by her friends, she sits on the stone floor in the living room and cuts cucumbers and carrots into strips. Beside her there is a glass of whisky, served, as it usually is in Mumbai, with water and

ice. It's early afternoon; the rationalists approach their meetings in a holiday spirit.

These gatherings are especially important for those who are threatened by loneliness in their traditional environment. Here, in secret, some, for the first time in their lives, find like-minded people and experience a sense of community. Here they talk about rejection by their families, how they hide their views in everyday life and avoid discussions on the subject, how they are unable to find partners. At the meetings the Brights try to share the burden of their sadness. Most were once Hindus, some Christians, a few Muslims. For the latter, they say, breaking away from the community is particularly dangerous. In the spring of 2017 a young ex-Muslim was hacked to death with machetes in the street because he had made a public declaration of atheism and set up a WhatsApp group for people of similar views. In Delhi, in June 2018, another young man had a report filed against him with the police and received death threats and eventually had to leave town because he posted on Facebook that Allah could not stop him from drinking a few beers with his friends.

Right: A Christian shrine in the fishing village of Worli near Mumbai.

'For the rationalists the next generation of free spirits is the source of high hopes, for, if the darkness doesn't fall all at once, then perhaps there is still time to put a stop to it.'

The rationalists' opponents spread fear. The new generation of non-believers is no longer prepared to bow to this. Instead of waiting for the next blow against reason, they now want to go on the offensive, and We the Brights has started a campaign to abolish Section 295a. In this they are supported by the human-rights lawyer Asim Sarode. The wording of the section is very vague and can be used against practically any joke, any flippant comment, thus violating freedom of speech and thought, says Sarode. Sanatan Sanstha and other radical Hindu groups have filed numerous charges against the lawyer and known rationalist, and he is currently under police protection. But the Brights do not want to get rid of Section 295a only; they are also demanding that other similar articles be more precisely worded and that a clearer definition of secularism be written into the Indian Constitution. In this way they hope to be able to fight the rise of fanatical groups of all religions in the future. 'We want to address the root causes of the problem. We want to clarify how much space there really is for freedom of speech and thought in modern India,' says Asim Sarode. He has consciously decided not to collaborate with established Indian rationalist organisations. 'They believe that, with the disenchantment of miracles, in the end one can convince everyone and end the violence. The new generation of rationalists and I want to force change through laws.'

Now the Brights want to persuade prominent figures to come out publicly as atheists. They raise funds to meet legal costs and they document stories of people who got into difficulties because of Section 295a. One of the cases they could take up might be that of Sanal Edamaruku, who remains in exile. If the Brights take the case and are successful, the guru-buster could finally return to India.

A sense of danger also hovers over the afternoon meeting in Worli. Amid all the irreverent talk about superstition and forging plans for the future, someone lays his hand on the shoulder of another of the attendees, who gets most agitated. 'They will kill him first!' All laugh loudly.

Chaitali Shinde comes alive when in the company of her friends. She has brought her daughter with her to the meeting; the eleven-year-old runs between the laughing adults. For Shinde and the other rationalists the next generation of free spirits is the source of high hopes, for, if the darkness doesn't fall all at once but seeps, drop by drop, into the midst of society, then perhaps there is still time to put a stop to it. Generations of rationalists have attempted to do so through discussion, education and changes in the law.

Maybe, says Chaitali Shinde, something more is needed to conjure up the brightness. She has named her child Amour: Love. 🐦

Left: A man prays at the entrance to a temple on the Manikarnika ghat, the principle site of funeral pyres in Varanasi.

Against Caste

Blinded by an idealised view of Indian culture, global public opinion struggles to condemn the caste system openly, even though it is a racist and discriminatory practice that to this day inflicts unspeakable injustices upon those at the bottom of the pile. Arundhati Roy looks at the situation in India and at the work of B.R. Ambedkar in his fight against caste-based social oppression in the 20th century.

ARUNDHATI ROY

Left: A group of Brahmins conducts a religious ceremony on the steps of one of the ghats in Varanasi.

'Annihilation of Caste' is the nearly eighty-year-old text of a speech that was never delivered. When I first read it I felt as though somebody had walked into a dim room and opened the windows. Reading Dr Bhimrao Ramji Ambedkar – who was a vocal critic of the caste system – bridges the gap between what most Indians are schooled to believe in and the reality we experience every day of our lives.

My father's family were Brahmo Samajis, a reformist sect. My father died a Christian. I never met him until I was an adult. I grew up with my mother in a Syrian Christian family in Ayemenem, a small village in communist-ruled Kerala. And yet all around me were the fissures and cracks of caste. Ayemenem had its own separate 'Paraiyar' church where 'Paraiyan' priests preached to an 'Untouchable' congregation. Caste was implied in people's names, in the way people referred to each other, in the work they did, in the clothes they wore, in the marriages that were arranged, in the language they spoke. Even so, I never encountered the notion of caste in a single school textbook. Reading Ambedkar alerted me to a gaping hole in our pedagogical universe. Reading him also made it clear why that hole exists and why it will continue to exist until Indian society undergoes radical, revolutionary change.

Revolutions can begin, and often have begun, with reading. If you have heard of Malala Yousafzai but not of Surekha Bhotmange, then do read Ambedkar.

Malala was only fifteen but had already committed several crimes. She was a girl, she lived in the Swat Valley in Pakistan, she was a BBC blogger, she was in a *New York Times* video, and she went to school. Malala wanted to be a doctor; her father wanted her to be a politician. She was a brave child. She (and her father) didn't take heed when the Taliban declared that schools were not meant for girls and threatened to kill her if she did not stop speaking out against them. On 9 October 2012, a gunman took her off her school bus and put a bullet through her head. Malala was flown to England, where, after receiving the best possible medical care, she survived. It was a miracle.

The US president and the secretary of state sent messages of support and solidarity. Madonna dedicated a song to her. Angelina Jolie wrote an article about her. Malala was nominated for the Nobel Peace Prize; she was on the cover of *Time*. Within days of the attempted assassination, Gordon Brown, former British prime minister and the UN Special Envoy for Global Education, launched an 'I am Malala' petition that called on the government of Pakistan to deliver education to every girl child. The US drone strikes in Pakistan continue with their feminist mission to 'take out' misogynist, Islamist terrorists.

Surekha Bhotmange was forty years old and had committed several crimes, too. She was a woman – an 'Untouchable' Dalit woman – who lived in India, and she wasn't dirt poor. She was more educated than her husband, so she functioned as the

ARUNDHATI ROY is the author of *The God of Small Things*, which won the Booker Prize in 1997, and *The Ministry of Utmost Happiness*, which was longlisted for the Man Booker Prize 2017. Both novels have been translated into more than forty languages. She has written several non-fiction books, including *Listening to Grasshoppers*, *Walking with the Comrades*, *Capitalism: A Ghost Story*, *Broken Republic*, *Things That Can and Cannot Be Said* and most recently *Azadi*. *My Seditious Heart*, a collection of her non-fiction, was published in 2019. Roy was born in 1959 in Shillong, India, and studied architecture in Delhi, where she now lives.

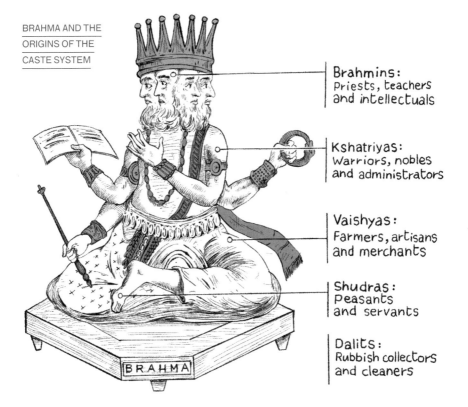

Brahmins:
Priests, teachers
and intellectuals

Kshatriyas:
Warriors, nobles
and administrators

Vaishyas:
Farmers, artisans
and merchants

Shudras:
Peasants
and servants

Dalits:
Rubbish collectors
and cleaners

BRAHMA

The caste system, with its Vedic origins (dating to around three thousand years ago), finds its source in the god of creation, Brahma. The Brahmin caste was drawn from his mouth, the Kshatriya from his arms, the Vaishya from his stomach and the Shudra from his feet. The Dalit caste was born from the dust that covered his feet. This description only covers the principal caste divisions – in reality, there are more than three thousand and at least as many subcastes.

head of her family. Dr Ambedkar was her hero. Like him, her family had renounced Hinduism and converted to Buddhism. Surekha's children were educated. Her two sons Sudhir and Roshan had been to college. Her daughter Priyanka was seventeen and finishing high school. Surekha and her husband had bought a little plot of land in the village of Khairlanji in the state of Maharashtra. It was surrounded by farms belonging to castes that considered themselves superior to the Mahar caste that Surekha belonged to. Because she was Dalit and had no right to aspire to a good life, the village *panchayat* did not permit her to get an electricity connection or turn her thatched mud hut into a brick house. The villagers would not allow her family to irrigate their fields with water from

'"To the Untouchables," Ambedkar said, with the sort of nerve that present-day intellectuals in India find hard to summon, "Hinduism is a veritable chamber of horrors."'

the canal or draw water from the public well. They tried to build a public road through her land, and when she protested they drove their bullock carts through her fields. They let their cattle loose to feed on her standing crop.

Still Surekha did not back down. She complained to the police, who paid no attention to her. Over the months, the tension in the village built to fever pitch. As a warning to her, the villagers attacked a relative of hers and left him for dead. She filed another police complaint. This time the police made some arrests, but the accused were released on bail almost immediately. At about six in the evening of the day they were released (29 September 2006), about seventy incensed villagers, men and women, arrived in tractors and surrounded the Bhotmanges' house. Her husband Bhaiyalal, who was out in the fields, heard the noise and ran home. He hid behind a bush and watched the mob attack his family. He ran to Dusala, the nearest town, and through a relative managed to call the police. (You need contacts to get the police to even pick up the phone.) They never came. The mob dragged Surekha, Priyanka and the two boys, one of them partially blind, out of the house. The boys were ordered to rape their mother and sister; when they refused, their genitals were mutilated, and eventually they were lynched. Surekha and Priyanka were gang-raped and beaten to death. The four bodies were dumped in a nearby canal, where they were found the next day.

At first, the press reported it as a 'morality' murder, suggesting that the villagers were upset because Surekha was having an affair with a relative (the man who had previously been assaulted). Mass protests by Dalit organisations eventually prodded the legal system into taking cognisance of the crime. Citizens' fact-finding committees reported how evidence had been tampered with and fudged. When the lower court finally pronounced a judgement, it sentenced the main perpetrators to death but refused to invoke the Scheduled Castes and Scheduled Tribes Prevention of Atrocities Act – the judge held that the Khairlanji massacre was a crime spurred by a desire for 'revenge'. He said there was no evidence of rape and no caste angle to the killing. For a judgement to weaken the legal framework in which it presents a crime, for which it then awards the death sentence, makes it easy for a higher court to eventually reduce, or even commute, the sentence. This is not uncommon practice in India. For a court to sentence people to death, however heinous their crime, can hardly be called just. For a court to acknowledge that caste prejudice continues to be a horrific reality in India would have counted as a gesture towards justice. Instead, the judge simply airbrushed caste out of the picture.

Surekha Bhotmange and her children lived in a market-friendly democracy. So there were no 'I am Surekha' petitions from the United Nations to the Indian government, nor any fiats or messages of outrage from heads of state. Which was just as well, because we don't want daisy-cutters dropped on us just because we practise caste.

'To the Untouchables,' Ambedkar said, with the sort of nerve that present-day intellectuals in India find hard to summon, 'Hinduism is a veritable chamber of horrors.'

For a writer to have to use terms like 'Untouchable', 'Scheduled Caste', 'Backward Class' and 'Other Backward Classes' to describe fellow human beings is like living in a chamber of horrors. Since Ambedkar used the word 'Untouchable' with a cold rage, and without flinching, so must I. Today 'Untouchable' has been substituted with the Marathi word '*Dalit*' (Broken People), which is, in turn, used interchangeably with 'Scheduled Caste'. This, as the scholar Rupa Viswanath points out, is incorrect practice, because the term 'Dalit' includes Untouchables who have converted to other religions to escape the stigma of caste (like the Paraiyars in my village who had converted to Christianity), whereas 'Scheduled Caste' does not. The official nomenclature of prejudice is a maze that can make everything read like a bigoted bureaucrat's file notings. To try and avoid this, I have mostly (though not always) used the word 'Untouchable' when I write about the past and 'Dalit' when I write about the present. When I write about Dalits who have converted to other religions, I specifically say Dalit Sikhs, Dalit Muslims or Dalit Christians.

Let me now return to Ambedkar's point about the chamber of horrors.

According to the National Crime Records Bureau, a crime is committed against a Dalit by a non-Dalit every sixteen minutes; every day, more than four Untouchable women are raped by Touchables; every week, thirteen Dalits are murdered and six Dalits are kidnapped. In 2012 alone, the year of the Delhi gang-rape and murder of a medical student, 1,574 Dalit women were raped (the rule of thumb is that only 10 per cent of rapes or other crimes against Dalits are ever reported) and 651 Dalits

Pages 112–13: A class at St Mary's, a school for children of the Untouchable caste in the Geeta Nagar district of Mumbai.

were murdered. That's just the rape and butchery. Not the stripping and parading naked, the forced shit-eating (literally), the seizing of land, the social boycotts, the restriction of access to drinking water. These statistics wouldn't include, say, Bant Singh of Punjab, a Mazhabi Dalit Sikh, who in 2005 had both his arms and a leg cleaved off for daring to file a case against the men who gang-raped his daughter. There are no separate statistics for triple amputees.

'If the fundamental rights are opposed by the community, no Law, no Parliament, no Judiciary can guarantee them in the real sense of the word,' said Ambedkar. 'What is the use of fundamental rights to the Negro in America, to the Jews in Germany and to the Untouchables in India? As Burke said, there is no method found for punishing the multitude.'

Ask any village policeman in India what his job is and he'll probably tell you it is to 'keep the peace'. That is done, most of the time, by upholding the caste system. Dalit aspirations are a breach of peace.

Annihilation of Caste is a breach of peace.

Other contemporary abominations like apartheid, racism, sexism, economic imperialism and religious fundamentalism have been politically and intellectually challenged at international forums. How is it that the practice of caste in India – one of the most brutal modes of hierarchical social organisation that human society has known – has managed to escape similar scrutiny and censure? Perhaps because it has come to be so fused with Hinduism, and by extension with so much that is seen to be kind and good – mysticism, spiritualism, non-violence, tolerance, vegetarianism, Gandhi, yoga, backpackers, the Beatles – that, at least to outsiders, it seems impossible to pry it loose and try to understand it.

To compound the problem, caste, unlike say apartheid, is not colour-coded and therefore not easy to see. Also unlike apartheid, the caste system has buoyant admirers in high places. They argue, quite openly, that caste is a social glue that binds as well as separates people and communities in interesting and, on the whole, positive ways. That it has given Indian society the strength and the flexibility to withstand the many challenges it has had to face. The Indian establishment blanches at the idea that discrimination and violence on the basis of caste can be compared to racism or to apartheid. It came down heavily on Dalits who tried to raise caste as an issue at the 2001 World Conference Against Racism in Durban, insisting that caste was an 'internal matter'. It showcased theses by well-known sociologists who argued at length that the practice of caste was not the same as racial discrimination and that caste was not the same as race. Ambedkar would have agreed with them. However, in the context of the Durban conference, the point Dalit activists were making was that though caste is not the same as race, casteism and racism are indeed comparable. Both are forms of discrimination that target people because of their descent. In solidarity with that sentiment, on 15 January 2014, at a public meeting on Capitol Hill in Washington, DC, commemorating Martin Luther King Jr's eighty-fifth birth anniversary, African Americans signed 'The Declaration of Empathy', which called for 'an end to the oppression of Dalits in India'.

In the current debates about identity and justice, growth and development, for many of the best-known Indian scholars, caste is at best a topic, a subheading, and, quite often, just a footnote. By force-fitting caste into reductive Marxist class analysis, the progressive and left-leaning Indian intelligentsia has made seeing caste even harder. This erasure, this Project of Unseeing, is sometimes a conscious political act and sometimes comes from a place of such rarefied privilege that caste has not been stumbled upon, not even in the dark, and therefore it is presumed to have been eradicated, like smallpox.

The origins of caste will continue to be debated by anthropologists for years to come, but its organising principles, based on a hierarchical, sliding scale of entitlements and duties, of purity and pollution, and the ways in which they were, and still are, policed and enforced, are not all that hard to understand. The top of the caste pyramid is considered pure and has plenty of entitlements. The bottom is considered polluted and has no entitlements but plenty of duties. The pollution–purity matrix is correlated to an

'The Indian establishment blanches at the idea that discrimination and violence on the basis of caste can be compared to racism or to apartheid. It came down heavily on Dalits who tried to raise caste as an issue at the 2001 World Conference Against Racism in Durban, insisting that caste was an "internal matter".'

Page 117: An Untouchable woman in a Buddhist temple in Mumbai; following a socio-political movement launched in 1956 by B.R. Ambedkar, many Untouchables converted to Buddhism.

elaborate system of caste-based, ancestral occupation. In 'Castes in India', a paper he wrote for a Columbia University seminar in 1916, Ambedkar defined a caste as an endogamous unit, an 'enclosed class'. On another occasion, he described the system as an 'ascending scale of reverence and a descending scale of contempt'.

What we call the caste system today is known in Hinduism's founding texts as 'varnashrama dharma' or 'chaturvarna', the system of four varnas. The approximately four thousand endogamous castes and subcastes (jatis) in Hindu society, each with its own specified hereditary occupation, are divided into four varnas – Brahmins (priests), Kshatriyas (soldiers), Vaishyas (traders) and Shudras (servants). Outside of these varnas are the avarna castes, the Ati-Shudras, subhumans, arranged in hierarchies of their own – the Untouchables, the Unseeables, the Unapproachables – whose presence, whose touch, whose very shadow is considered to be polluting by privileged-caste Hindus. In some communities, to prevent inbreeding, each endogamous caste is divided into exogamous gotras. Exogamy is then policed with as much ferocity as endogamy – with beheadings and lynchings that have the approval of the community elders. Each region of India has lovingly perfected its own unique version of caste-based cruelty, based on an unwritten code that is much worse than the Jim Crow laws. In addition to being forced to live in segregated settlements, Untouchables were not allowed to use the public roads that privileged castes used, they were not allowed to drink from common wells, they were not allowed into Hindu temples, they were not allowed into privileged-caste schools, they were not permitted to cover their upper bodies, they were only allowed to wear certain kinds of clothes and certain kinds of jewellery. Some castes, like the Mahars, the caste to which Ambedkar belonged, had to tie brooms to their waists to sweep away their polluted footprints, others had to hang spittoons around their necks to collect their polluted saliva. Men of the privileged castes had undisputed rights over the bodies of Untouchable women. Love is polluting. Rape is pure. In many parts of India, much of this continues to this day.

What remains to be said about an imagination, human or divine, that has thought up a social arrangement such as this?

As if the dharma of varnashrama were not enough, there is also the burden of karma. Those born into the subordinated castes are supposedly being punished for the bad deeds they have done in their past lives. In effect, they are living out a prison sentence. Acts of insubordination could lead to an enhanced sentence, which would mean another cycle of rebirth as an Untouchable or as a Shudra. So it's best to behave.

'There cannot be a more degrading system of social organization than the caste system,' said Ambedkar. 'It is the system that deadens, paralyzes and cripples the people from helpful activity.'

The most famous Indian in the world, Mohandas Karamchand Gandhi, disagreed. He believed that caste represented the genius of Indian society. At a speech at a missionary conference in Madras in 1916, he said:

The vast organisation of caste answered not only the religious wants of the

Fewer than 3 per cent of Dalits have a university degree, but often even those who escape the limiting traditions of rural India to further their education encounter caste discrimination in the top academies. Bullied, isolated and humiliated by their peers and professors, many can't bear the climate of intimidation and – despite the enormous effort it has taken to get themselves in a position to study – decide to take their own lives. In recent years several prominent cases have shaken public opinion: Jaspreet Singh, a medical student in Chandigarh, Punjab, who hanged himself after he was repeatedly told by the head of his department that he would never be allowed to become a doctor; Rohith Vemula, who took his own life after he was suspended from the University of Hyderabad because of his activism as part of the Ambedkar Student Association, leaving behind a searing letter of accusation; Payal Tadvi, an Adivasi and newly graduated gynaecologist from Maharashtra, who was harassed by her higher-caste colleagues and found her work obstructed at the hospital. In India a student takes their own life every hour – the issue is increasingly alarming and does not apply solely to caste discrimination. The other large problem is academic stress and the enormous pressure that weighs down the universities. In 2014 the director Abhay Kumar shot an acclaimed documentary, *Placebo*, about the crisis of anxiety and depression among the students at the All India Institute of Medical Sciences, which has an acceptance rate of 0.1 per cent – by comparison, getting into Harvard (7 per cent) or MIT (9 per cent) is a walk in the park. The suicide rate for young men aged between fifteen and twenty-nine is one of the highest in the world, as is that for women, who make up about one-third of Indians who take their own lives.

community, but it answered too its political needs. The villagers managed their internal affairs through the caste system, and through it they dealt with any oppression from the ruling power or powers. It is not possible to deny the organising capability of a nation that was capable of producing the caste system its wonderful power of organisation.

In 1921, in his Gujarati journal *Navajivan*, he wrote:

I believe that if Hindu Society has been able to stand, it is because it is founded on the caste system ... To destroy the caste system and adopt the Western European social system means that Hindus must give up the principle of hereditary occupation which is the soul of the caste system. Hereditary principle is an eternal principle. To change it is to create disorder. I have no use for a Brahmin if I cannot call him a Brahmin for my life. It will be chaos if every day a Brahmin is changed into a Shudra and a Shudra is to be changed into a Brahmin.

Though Gandhi was an admirer of the caste system, he believed that there should be no hierarchy between castes, that all castes should be considered equal and that the avarna castes, the Ati-Shudras, should be brought into the varna system. Ambedkar's response to this was that 'the outcaste is a by-product of the caste system. There will be outcastes as long as there are castes. Nothing can emancipate the outcaste except the destruction of the caste system.'

It has been almost seventy years since the August 1947 transfer of power between the imperial British government and the government of India. Is caste in the past?

THE PASSENGER   Arundhati Roy

Left: A *dabbawala* hoists a load
of tiffin boxes in Mumbai. Every
day an estimated 200,000 meals
are delivered to workplaces by the
dabbawala service.

How does varnashrama dharma play out in our new 'democracy'?

A lot has changed. India has had a Dalit president and even a Dalit chief justice. The rise of political parties dominated by Dalits and other subordinated castes is a remarkable, and in some ways a revolutionary, development. Even if the form it has taken is that a small but visible minority – the leadership – lives out the dreams of the vast majority, given our history, the aggressive assertion of Dalit pride in the political arena can only be a good thing. The complaints about corruption and callousness brought against parties like the Bahujan Samaj Party (BSP) apply to the older political parties on an even larger scale, but charges levelled against the BSP take on a shriller, more insulting tone because its leader is someone like Mayawati, four-term chief minister of Uttar Pradesh – a Dalit, a single woman, and unapologetic about being both. Whatever the BSP's failings may be, its contribution towards building Dalit dignity is an immense political task that ought never to be minimised. The worry is that even as subordinated castes are becoming a force to reckon with in parliamentary democracy, democracy itself is being undermined in serious and structural ways.

After the fall of the Soviet Union, India, which was once at the forefront of the Non-Aligned Movement, repositioned itself as a 'natural ally' of the United States and Israel. In the 1990s, the Indian government embarked on a process of dramatic economic reforms, opening up a previously protected market to global capital, with natural resources, essential services and national infrastructure that had been developed over fifty years with public money now turned over to private corporations. Twenty years later, despite a spectacular GDP growth rate (which has recently slowed down), the new economic policies have led to the concentration of wealth in fewer and fewer hands. Today, India's one hundred richest people own assets equivalent to one-fourth of its celebrated GDP. In a nation of 1.2 billion, more than 800 million people live on less than twenty rupees (forty cents) a day. Giant corporations virtually own and run the country. Politicians and political parties have begun to function as subsidiary holdings of big business.

How has this affected traditional caste networks? Some argue that caste has insulated Indian society and prevented it from fragmenting and atomising like Western society did after the Industrial Revolution. Others argue the opposite; they say that the unprecedented levels of urbanisation and the creation of a new work environment have shaken up the old order and rendered caste hierarchies irrelevant if not obsolete. Both claims deserve serious attention. Pardon the somewhat unliterary interlude that follows, but generalisations cannot replace facts.

A recent list of dollar billionaires published by *Forbes* magazine features fifty-five Indians. The figures, naturally, are based on revealed wealth. Even among these dollar billionaires the distribution of wealth is a steep pyramid in which the cumulative wealth of the top ten outstrips the forty-five below them. Seven out of those top ten are Vaishyas, all of them CEOs of major corporations with business interests all over the world. Between them they own and operate ports, mines,

'In big business and small, in agriculture as well as industry, caste and capitalism have blended into a disquieting, uniquely Indian alloy. Cronyism is built into the caste system.'

oil fields, gas fields, shipping companies, pharmaceutical companies, telephone networks, petrochemical plants, aluminium plants, cellphone networks, television channels, fresh food outlets, high schools, film production companies, stem cell storage systems, electricity supply networks and Special Economic Zones. They are: Mukesh Ambani (Reliance Industries Ltd), Lakshmi Mittal (Arcelor Mittal), Dilip Shanghvi (Sun Pharmaceuticals), the Ruia brothers (Ruia Group), K.M. Birla (Aditya Birla Group), Savitri Devi Jindal (O.P. Jindal Group), Gautam Adani (Adani Group) and Sunil Mittal (Bharti Airtel). Of the remaining forty-five, nineteen are Vaishyas, too. The rest are for the most part Parsis, Bohras and Khattris (all mercantile castes) and Brahmins. There are no Dalits or Adivasis in this list.

Apart from big business, Banias (Vaishyas) continue to have a firm hold on small trade in cities and on traditional rural moneylending across the country, which has millions of impoverished peasants and Adivasis, including those who live deep in the forests of Central India, caught in a spiralling debt trap. The tribal-dominated states in India's north-east – Arunachal Pradesh, Manipur, Mizoram, Tripura, Meghalaya, Nagaland and Assam – have, since 'Independence', witnessed decades of insurgency, militarisation and bloodshed. Through all this, Marwari and Bania traders have settled there, kept a low profile and consolidated their businesses. They now control almost all the economic activity in the region.

In the 1931 census, which was the last to include caste as an aspect of the survey, Vaishyas accounted for 2.7 per cent of the population (while the Untouchables accounted for 12.5 per cent). Given their access to better healthcare and more secure futures for their children, the figure for Vaishyas is likely to have decreased rather than increased. Either way, their economic clout in the new economy is extraordinary. In big business and small, in agriculture as well as industry, caste and capitalism have blended into a disquieting, uniquely Indian alloy. Cronyism is built into the caste system.

Vaishyas are only doing their divinely ordained duty. The *Arthashastra* (*c.* 350 BCE) says usury is the Vaishya's right. The *Manusmriti* (*c.* 150 CE) goes further and suggests a sliding scale of interest rates: 2 per cent per month for Brahmins, 3 per cent for Kshatriyas, 4 per cent for Vaishyas and 5 per cent for Shudras. On an annual basis, the Brahmin was to pay 24 per cent interest and the Shudra and Dalit 60 per cent. Even today, for moneylenders to charge a desperate farmer or landless labourer an annual interest of 60 per cent (or more) for a loan is quite normal. If they cannot pay in cash, they have to pay what is known as 'bodily interest', which means they are expected to toil for the moneylender from generation to generation to repay impossible debts. It goes without saying that according to the *Manusmriti* no one can be forced into the service of anyone belonging to a 'lower' caste.

Vaishyas control Indian business. What

do the Brahmins – the bhudevas (gods on earth) – do? The 1931 census puts their population at 6.4 per cent, but, like the Vaishyas and for similar reasons, that percentage, too, has probably declined. According to a survey by the Centre for the Study of Developing Societies (CSDS), from having a disproportionately high number of representatives in Parliament, Brahmins have seen their numbers drop dramatically. Does this mean Brahmins have become less influential?

According to Ambedkar, Brahmins, who were 3 per cent of the population in the Madras Presidency in 1948, held 37 per cent of the gazetted posts and 43 per cent of the non-gazetted posts in government jobs. There is no longer a reliable way to keep track of these trends because after 1931 the Project of Unseeing set in. In the absence of information that ought to be available, we have to make do with what we can find. In a 1990 piece called 'Brahmin Power', the writer Khushwant Singh observed:

Brahmins form no more than 3.5 per cent of the population of our country … today they hold as much as 70 per cent of government jobs. I presume the figure refers only to gazetted posts. In the senior echelons of the civil service from the rank of deputy secretaries upward, out of 500 there are 310 Brahmins, i.e. 63 per cent; of the 26 state chief secretaries, 19 are Brahmins; of the 27 Governors and Lt Governors, 13 are Brahmins; of the 16 Supreme Court Judges, 9 are Brahmins; of the 330 judges of High Courts, 166 are Brahmins; of 140 ambassadors, 58 are Brahmins; of the total 3,300 IAS officers, 2,376 are Brahmins. They do equally well in electoral posts; of the 508 Lok Sabha members, 190 were Brahmins; of 244 in the Rajya Sabha, 89

are Brahmins. These statistics clearly prove that this 3.5 per cent of Brahmin community of India holds between 36 per cent to 63 per cent of all the plum jobs available in the country. How this has come about I do not know. But I can scarcely believe that it is entirely due to the Brahmin's higher IQ.

The statistics Khushwant Singh cites may be flawed, but they are unlikely to be drastically flawed. They are a quarter of a century old now. Some new census-based information would help but is unlikely to be forthcoming.

According to the CSDS study, 47 per cent of all Supreme Court chief justices between 1950 and 2000 were Brahmins. During the same period, 40 per cent of the associate justices in the high courts and lower courts were Brahmin. The Backward Classes Commission, in a 2007 report, said that 37.17 per cent of the Indian bureaucracy was made up of Brahmins. Most of them occupied the top posts.

Brahmins have also traditionally dominated the media. Here too, what Ambedkar said in 1945 still has resonance:

The Untouchables have no Press. The Congress Press is closed to them and is determined not to give them the slightest publicity. They cannot have their own Press and for obvious reasons. No paper can survive without advertisement revenue. Advertisement revenue can come only from business and in India all business, both high and small, is attached to the Congress and will not

Page 124: A guest at a wedding at the Wilson Gymkhana on the seafront of Marine Drive in Mumbai.
Page 125: A man poses in a doorway in Dharavi, a Mumbai slum.

THE PASSENGER   Arundhati Roy

AGAINST GANDHI

This article is an extract from 'The Doctor and the Saint', Arundhati Roy's introduction to a book by B.R. Ambedkar, *Annihilation of Caste* (first published in 1936 and currently published internationally in English by Verso Books). Roy praises Ambedkar's battle against Untouchability, setting it against the example of Gandhi, whose position on caste seems to have been far more ambivalent. In Gandhi's idealised vision of rural, primitive India, caste played an important social role. Although Gandhi did embrace the cause of the Untouchables later in his life, his attitude was tinged with the paternalism typical of caste reformers from privileged backgrounds, who offered charity and solidarity without actually disturbing the status quo. Gandhi was aware of the powerful symbolism of a privileged person renouncing his privilege, as he did when he wore the clothes of a poor man, and he knew how this could capture the popular imagination. According to Roy, though, 'The battle of the poor and the powerless is one of reclamation, not renunciation', and when the Untouchables demanded rights, Gandhi did not support them, even though they used *satyagraha*, the very weapon that he himself forged to resist the British. He didn't back their struggle to create their own political organisations and elect representatives and condemned the street-cleaners' strike. 'The fact is there was never much daylight between Gandhi's views on caste and those of the Hindu right.' Roy sees this as another facet of the racism expressed by Gandhi towards black people during his year in South Africa, when he fought for Indians to have the same rights as the British but wanted increased segregation for black people.

favour any Non-Congress organisation. The staff of the Associated Press in India, which is the main news distributing agency in India, is entirely drawn from the Madras Brahmins – indeed the whole of the Press in India is in their hands – and they, for well-known reasons, are entirely pro-Congress and will not allow any news hostile to the Congress to get publicity. These are reasons beyond the control of the Untouchables.

In 2006, the CSDS did a survey on the social profile of New Delhi's media elite. Of the 315 key decision makers surveyed from thirty-seven Delhi-based Hindi and English publications and television channels, almost 90 per cent of the decision makers in the English language print media and 79 per cent in television were found to be 'upper caste'. Of them, 49 per cent were Brahmins. Not one of the 315 was a Dalit or an Adivasi; only 4 per cent belonged to castes designated as Shudra, and 3 per cent were Muslim (who make up 13.4 per cent of the population).

That's the journalists and the 'media personalities'. Who owns the big media houses that they work for? Of the four most important English national dailies, three are owned by Vaishyas and one by a Brahmin family concern. The Times Group (Bennett, Coleman and Company Ltd), the largest mass media company in India, whose holdings include *The Times of India* and the twenty-four-hour news channel Times Now, is owned by the Jain family (Banias). The *Hindustan Times* is owned by the Bhartiyas, who are Marwari Banias; the *Indian Express* by the

Goenkas, also Marwari Banias; the *Hindu* is owned by a Brahmin family concern; the *Dainik Jagran* Hindi daily, which is the largest-selling newspaper in India with a circulation of fifty-five million, is owned by the Gupta family, Banias from Kanpur. *Dainik Bhaskar*, among the most influential Hindi dailies with a circulation of 17.5 million, is owned by Agarwals, Banias again. Reliance Industries Ltd (owned by Mukesh Ambani, a Gujarati Bania) has controlling shares in twenty-seven major national and regional TV channels. The Zee TV network, one of the largest national TV news and entertainment networks, is owned by Subhash Chandra, also a Bania. (In southern India, caste manifests itself somewhat differently. For example, the Eenadu Group – which owns newspapers, the largest film city in the world and a dozen TV channels, among other things – is headed by Ramoji Rao of the Kamma peasant caste of Andhra Pradesh, which bucks the trend of Brahmin–Bania ownership of Big Media. Another major media house, the Sun TV group, is owned by the Marans, who are designated as a 'backward' caste but are politically powerful today.)

After Independence, in an effort to right a historic wrong, the Indian government implemented a policy of reservation (positive discrimination) in universities and for jobs in state-run bodies for those who belong to Scheduled Castes and Scheduled Tribes. Reservation is the only opportunity the Scheduled Castes have to break into the mainstream. (Of course, the policy does not apply to Dalits who have converted to other religions but continue to face discrimination.) To be eligible for the reservation policy, a Dalit needs to have completed high school. According to government data, 71.3 per cent of Scheduled Caste students drop out before they matriculate, which means that even for low-end government jobs,

'There are (officially) 1.3 million people, mostly women, who continue to earn their living by carrying baskets of human shit on their heads as they clean out traditional-style toilets that use no water.'

the reservation policy only applies to one in every four Dalits. The minimum qualification for a white-collar job is a graduate degree. According to the 2001 census, only 2.24 per cent of the Dalit population are graduates. The policy of reservation, however minuscule the percentage of the Dalit population it applies to, has nevertheless given Dalits an opportunity to find their way into public services, to become doctors, scholars, writers, judges, policemen and officers of the civil services. Their numbers are small, but the fact that there is some Dalit representation in the echelons of power alters old social equations. It creates situations that were unimaginable even a few decades ago in which, say, a Brahmin clerk may have to serve under a Dalit civil servant. Even this tiny opportunity that Dalits have won for themselves washes up against a wall of privileged-caste hostility.

The National Commission for Scheduled Castes and Scheduled Tribes, for example, reports that in Central Public Sector Enterprises, only 8.4 per cent of the A-Grade officers (pardon the horrible term) belong to the Scheduled Castes, when the figure should be 15 per cent.

The same report has some disturbing statistics about the representation of Dalits and Adivasis in India's judicial services: among Delhi's twenty high court judges, not one belonged to the Scheduled Castes, and in all other judicial posts, the figure was 1.2 per cent; similar figures were reported from Rajasthan; Gujarat had no Dalit or Adivasi judges; in Tamil Nadu, with its legacy of social justice movements, only

four out of thirty-eight high court judges were Dalit; Kerala, with its Marxist legacy, had one Dalit high court judge among twenty-five. A study of the prison population would probably reveal an inverse ratio.

Former President K.R. Narayanan, a Dalit himself, was mocked by the judicial fraternity when he suggested that Scheduled Castes and Scheduled Tribes, who according to the 2011 census make up 25 per cent of India's 1.2 billion population, should find proportionate representation as judges in the Supreme Court. 'Eligible persons from these categories are available and their under-representation or non-representation would not be justifiable,' he said in 1999. 'Any reservation in judiciary is a threat to its independence and the rule of law,' was the response of a senior Supreme Court advocate. Another high-profile legal luminary said: 'Job quotas are a vexed subject now. I believe the primacy of merit must be maintained.'

'Merit' is the weapon of choice for an Indian elite that has dominated a system by allegedly divine authorisation and denied knowledge – of certain kinds – to the subordinated castes for thousands of years. Now that it is being challenged, there have been passionate privileged-caste protests against the policy of reservation in government jobs and student quotas in universities. The presumption is that 'merit' exists in an ahistorical social vacuum and that the advantages that come from privileged-caste social networking and the establishment's entrenched hostility towards the subordinated castes are not

Ambedkar is seen as the father of the 1949 Indian Constitution, the first in the country's history to introduce positive discrimination through a system of quotas for the most disadvantaged castes, mainly Dalits and Adivasis. This meant that groups historically subject to discrimination were now guaranteed representation in universities, public administration and government. In the 1980s a parliamentary commission named after its president, B.P. Mandal, produced a clearer definition of what constituted poverty, with the aim of extending the quotas to other disadvantaged castes. This came into effect in the decade that followed but caused anger among people in higher castes, who wanted the quotas to be based on economic or meritocratic criteria. In some states, such as Tamil Nadu, quotas were as high as 69 per cent of posts in public administration and education, and many Brahmins used fake birth certificates to pass themselves off as Dalits. The Supreme Court subsequently ruled that no more than 50 per cent of posts should be allocated according to positive discrimination. Nevertheless, the system remained controversial, and in 2015 fierce protests broke out in Gujarat, initiated by the Patels, a caste of seemingly relatively well-off people who wanted to be included among the protected groups. So it was that in 2019 Prime Minister Modi met some of these demands by promising a 10 per cent share of the quotas to the poorest people among higher castes, a shift that reopened debate on the system as a whole.

factors that deserve consideration. In truth, 'merit' has become a euphemism for nepotism.

In Jawaharlal Nehru University (JNU) – which is regarded as a bastion of progressive social scientists and historians – only 3.29 per cent of the faculty is Dalit and 1.44 per cent Adivasi, while the quotas are meant to be 15 per cent and 7.5 per cent, respectively. This, despite having supposedly implemented reservation for twenty-seven years. In 2010, when the subject was raised, some of its professors emeritus said that implementing the constitutionally mandated reservation policy would 'prevent JNU from remaining one of the premier centres of excellence'. They argued that if reservation was implemented in faculty positions at JNU, 'the well-to-do will move to foreign and private universities, and the disadvantaged will no longer be able to get world class education which JNU has been so proud to offer them so far'. B.N. Mallick, a professor of life sciences, was less shy: 'Some castes are genetically malnourished and so very little can be achieved in raising them up; and if they are, it would be undoing excellence and merit.' Year after year, privileged-caste students have staged mass protests against reservation across India.

That's the news from the top. At the other end of New India, the Sachar Committee Report tells us that Dalits and Adivasis still remain at the bottom of the economic pyramid where they always were, below the Muslim community. We know that Dalits and Adivasis make up the majority of the millions of people displaced by mines, dams and other major infrastructure projects. They are the pitifully low-paid farm workers and the contract labourers who work in the urban construction industry. Seventy per cent of Dalits are by and large landless. In states like Punjab,

Bihar, Haryana and Kerala, the figure is as high as 90 per cent.

There is one government department in which Dalits are over-represented by a factor of six. Almost 90 per cent of those designated as sweepers – who clean streets, who go down manholes and service the sewage system, who clean toilets and do menial jobs – and employed by the government of India are Dalits. (Even this sector is up for privatisation now, which means private companies will be able to subcontract jobs on a temporary basis to Dalits for less pay and with no guarantee of job security.)

While janitors' jobs in malls and in corporate offices with swanky toilets that do not involve 'manual scavenging' go to non-Dalits, there are (officially) 1.3 million people, mostly women, who continue to earn their living by carrying baskets of human shit on their heads as they clean out traditional-style toilets that use no water. Though it is against the law, the Indian Railways is one of the biggest employers of manual scavengers. Its 14,300 trains transport 25 million passengers across 65,000 kilometres every day. Their shit is funnelled straight on to the railway tracks through 172,000 open-discharge toilets. This shit, which must amount to several tons a day, is cleaned by hand, without gloves or any protective equipment, exclusively by Dalits. While the Prohibition of Employment as Manual Scavengers and Their Rehabilitation Bill, 2012, was cleared by the Cabinet and by the Rajya Sabha in September 2013, the Indian Railways has ignored it. With deepening poverty and the steady evaporation of government jobs, a section of Dalits has to fiercely guard its 'permanent' state employment as hereditary shit-cleaners against predatory interlopers.

A few Dalits have managed to overcome

these odds. Their personal stories are extraordinary and inspirational. Some Dalit businessmen and women have come together to form their own institution, the Dalit Indian Chamber of Commerce and Industry, which is praised and patronised by big business and given plenty of play on television and big media because it helps to give the impression that as long as you work hard, capitalism is intrinsically egalitarian.

Time was when a caste Hindu crossing the oceans was said to have lost caste and become polluted. Now, the caste system is up for export. Wherever Hindus go, they take it with them. It exists among the brutalised Tamils in Sri Lanka; it exists among upwardly mobile Indian immigrants in the 'Free World', in Europe as well as in the United States. For about ten years, Dalit-led groups in the UK have been lobbying to have caste discrimination recognised by British law as a form of racial discrimination. Caste-Hindu lobbies have managed to scuttle it for the moment.

Democracy hasn't eradicated caste. It has entrenched and modernised it. This is why it's time to read Ambedkar. (2014) 🖋

This is an extract from 'The Doctor and the Saint', Arundhati Roy's 2014 introduction to B.R. Ambedkar's *Annihilation of Caste: The Annotated Critical Edition* (Navayana, India / Verso Books, USA, UK), reprinted in *My Seditious Heart: Collected Non-Fiction* (Haymarket Books, 2019 USA / Hamish Hamilton, 2019 UK, India), in which volume readers can find citations and sources for the information in this piece.

Cut to Switzerland!

JUHI SAKLANI

Dilwale Dulhaniya Le Jayenge ('The Big-
Hearted Will Whisk Away the Bride'),
a Bollywood film from 1995, which took
place, in part, in Switzerland, is projected
at the Maratha Mandir cinema in Mumbai.

Switzerland is the embodiment of Bollywood's passion for exotic locations, a trend that began in the 1960s and seems unlikely to lose its appeal any time soon. For modern Indians, what is evoked by the phrase 'foreign country' has changed over time, along with the Indian public's self-image, but Switzerland continues to reap the benefits of an Indian fascination with the Alpine country.

Back in 1962 producer, director, actor Raj Kapoor, the grand showman of Hindi films – the term Bollywood had not been coined yet – was planning his first movie to be shot in colour. It was to be an intense saga with operatic emotions. Big-name stars, music guaranteed to be wildly popular and the expensive technology of Technicolor were all in place. But what could he present as the unique never-before-seen feature of his labour of love? Extensive scenes of famous European locations was his solution.

Raj Kapoor's *Sangam* ('Confluence', 1964) was not the first Hindi film to be shot outside India. Experiments with filming abroad had been made for a few productions such as *India in Africa* (1939) and *Singapore* (1960), but these films had not been able to capitalise on the novelty. With *Sangam*, however, the glamour of the 'foreign' burst upon the Indian silver screen. Raj Kapoor spent a good half an hour depicting the lead pair's honeymoon in Europe, although these sequences had nothing much to add to the central plot. The hero and heroine romanced in Venetian gondolas, shopped in Paris, walked in Rome, sledged in Switzerland ... As his heroine Vyjayanthimala said years later in an interview, 'it was like a documentary'.

But the documentary worked. *Sangam* was the highest-earning film to come out of Bombay that year, and a lot of credit for that was given to the appeal of the foreign locales.

'FOREIGNCOUNTRY'

The 'foreign' land. A place other than one's own. A theatre of beauty, adventure, discovery. At times a stage for self-exploration. And, if you were living in the India of the 1960s, a concept so dream-like that you could hardly even desire it.

The kind of money required to afford international travel was well out of reach for all but the smallest urban elite in a country which had recently become independent from British colonial rule in 1948 and was a low-income socialist economy. In my childhood in the 1970s, when Hindi-speaking people discussed someone who had gone abroad (usually for a job), if they forgot the name of the place they would simply say 'foreigncountry' as if it were one word. Or they would just say 'foreign'. 'That actor has gone to foreign for his honeymoon.' 'Our uncle is going to foreigncountry for work.' When such uncles brought back a gift, say a dress or a small bottle of perfume, it was treasured for years and only used on special occasions.

No surprises that the huge success of

JUHI SAKLANI is a writer and photographer whose articles on travel, cinema and contemporary life and culture in India have been published in major Indian newspapers, magazines and online. She is the author of *Gandhi* (Dorling Kindersley, 2014) and *Filmi Escapes* (Lonely Planet, 2013) and runs the Facebook page FilmShuru. In 2019 she won the Photosphere fellowship from the India Habitat Centre, Delhi.

'The "foreign" land. A place other than one's own. A theatre of beauty, adventure, discovery. At times a stage for self-exploration. And, if you were living in the India of the 1960s, a concept so dream-like that you could hardly even desire it.'

Sangam was ascribed in large part to its 'foreign' scenes. No surprises either that in a film industry always looking for a formula for success, *Sangam* spawned a whole generation of imitators. The 1960s saw a spate of films which not only showcased foreign locations but were carefully given titles that left no one in any doubt about their glamorous content: *Love in Tokyo* (1966), *An Evening in Paris* (1967), *Around the World* (1967), *Night in London* (1967), *Spy in Rome* (1969) all tried to capitalise on well-known hot spots of international glamour in the recently adopted, affordable technology of Eastmancolor.

On-screen pairs romancing abroad also fitted nicely into the new, rather glamorous direction Hindi cinema had taken in the 1960s. Emerging from an era of predominantly black-and-white films, which tried to reflect India's grim rural realities or the struggles of its urban underclass, colour films now started showing Westernised, English-speaking characters with fashionable clothes and flashy sports cars. Going abroad and having fun fitted well with this light-hearted mood.

Filmmakers tried to formulate stories that would justify this kind of shooting – and sometimes didn't even try too hard! In *An Evening in Paris* the heroine is a rich heiress who has had her heart broken so often in India that she is fed up with Indian men and – for no logical reason we can discern – goes to Paris to look for her true love! 'Look, look, look, look, an evening in Paris' goes the title song, underlining the film's agenda. Meanwhile, *Love in Tokyo* had the hero visiting Japan to bring back his dead brother's son; the brother had married a Japanese girl and had been disowned by their traditionally orthodox mother. This set the scene for romantic sequences in Tokyo and a famous Hindi song that went 'Sayonara Sayonara'.

'Around the World in 8 Dollars' was the title song of *Around the World*, India's first seventy-millimetre Technicolor film, which simply had the hero travelling around the world on a shoestring budget and a very thin plotline. He is a rich man, invited by a family friend to embark on a world tour, but, thanks to the jealous villain, he is stranded in Japan with only eight dollars (eight dollars being the amount of foreign exchange that the then Indian government permitted tourists travelling abroad to take out of the country). Yet he persists in finishing his tour. The song celebrates 'glamorous Los Angeles', 'the golden colours of Rome, 'the singing waves of Venice' laid over utterly random shots of Niagara Falls, Swiss ski slopes and colourful fountains.

When several such films did not succeed, the formula was soon given up. In the 1970s foreign locales receded into the background as notable films focused on societal power structures and political frustration. The towering figure of the 1970s, the legendary actor Amitabh Bachchan, played enraged heroes who had neither the social standing nor the money to travel abroad, nor did they have time for light-hearted romances in Paris. Eventually, the reintroduction of the foreign locale to the

'An essential element of 20th-century Bollywood, the Dream Sequence, usually unfolded with the actors running in slow motion, singing a melodious love song ... No self-respecting fantasy song took place anywhere except in Switzerland.'

Bollywood screen came thanks to the one man who can be called both a pillar of the idea we call Bollywood and the godfather of the Swiss shoot: Yash Chopra.

NOW ... CUT TO SWITZERLAND

Having just had an encounter with her lover, whom she hasn't chastely married yet (or whom she loves silently), the heroine retreats to her room, closes her eyes and we know that it is time for that essential element of 20th-century Bollywood: the Dream Sequence. Dream sequences usually unfolded with the actors running in slow motion, singing a melodious love song, the heroine wearing saris and scarves that would flutter in the breeze. But no self-respecting fantasy song took place anywhere except in Switzerland.

No one did these songs better than producer-director Yash Chopra. Chopra was a Bollywood colossus who, by the time of his death in 2012, had produced fifty movies in his long career, many of them blockbusters. He directed films critiquing social conservatism in the 1960s and intense action dramas in the 1970s, but he is really remembered for his films that gave a lasting image to romance in India – and Switzerland was a key ingredient in his recipe. Snow-covered peaks, jewel-like lakes, sheep grazing in meadows straight out of a pastoral fantasy, all repeatedly provided a backdrop for heroes and heroines who came running towards each other as if the romantic impulse could not be physically contained any longer and burst into song-and-dance

to give vent to their feelings. After nearly three decades of including such scenes in his films, Chopra was named the honorary ambassador to the Swiss town of Interlaken in 2011, where a statue of him was unveiled in 2016, while his beloved lake, Lauenensee, near Gstaad, where many of his films were shot, was unofficially renamed Yash Chopra Lake after him.

Chopra had famously shot in the Keukenhof Tulip Gardens near Amsterdam for the title song of his film *Silsila* ('A Series of Events', 1981), but after his picturisation of Switzerland in the movie *Chandni* ('Moonlight', 1989) became a runaway success, he never looked back. In *Chandni*, the eponymous heroine, played by Sridevi, fantasises about romancing her lover in the Alps. In *Darr* ('Fear', 1993), heroine Juhi Chawla, thrilled that her fiancé has bought a house for her, opens the back door and runs out singing – straight into Switzerland! In *Dil to Paagal Hai* ('The Heart is Crazy', 1997), the shy Madhuri Dixit expresses her romantic feelings by swaying gently to a song in the meadows of Switzerland.

Chopra opened the floodgates for both tourists and other filmmakers. Film journalist Anupama Chopra wrote in 1996: 'Pity Saroj Khan. Bollywood's hottest choreographer has just returned from Switzerland – her sixth trip in five months. "Looking at the mountains," Khan says, "is torture now!"'

Back in the 1990s film scripts would routinely include the instruction 'Cut to Switzerland', and film crews used to squeeze

Above and below: The set of the soap opera *Kundali Bhagya* ('The Fate of Our Stars') in a Bollywood studio in Mumbai.

Above: On the set of the soap opera *Kundali Bhagya*.

THE PASSENGER   Juhi Saklani

With their roots in ancient Indian epic and influences ranging from Parsee theatre to Hollywood musicals and MTV, Bollywood films have been India's main cultural export over the last twenty years, a weapon of soft power that shifts the country's image away from Western stereotypes of poverty and underdevelopment and reshapes the identities of Indians themselves. Bollywood overtook Hollywood in terms of box-office sales in 2004 (although its revenue is lower because tickets are cheaper), and it produces around twice as many films. The term Bollywood was coined in the 1970s to describe films produced in Hindi and thus doesn't include the rich cinematic traditions of the rest of India. It covers a variety of genres, from realism to 'dacoit' films, rather like westerns. The films that have come to define Bollywood in much of the world are the so-called 'masalas', a blend of romantic comedy, action and melodrama – just as masala in Indian cuisine is a mixture of different spices. Music and dance are essential elements in these films, and the soundtrack can be a deciding factor in their success. They are filmed in Hindustani, a language derived from Hindi–Urdu and spoken in both India and Pakistan. The distribution of Indian films in Pakistan is strictly limited, but Indian stars still have a huge following there: in the 1990s Pakistani cricket fans had a special chant in honour of the actor Madhuri Dixit: '*Madhuri dedo, Kashmir lelo!*' – 'Give us Madhuri, take Kashmir!'

in their shots in popular Swiss locations, trying not to get in each other's way.

In 2012 an ageing Yash Chopra made his last film, *Jab Tak Hai Jaan* ('As Long as I Live'). Although it was mostly shot in London, the director wanted to picturise the title song in his favourite country, but he passed away towards the end of making the film, and the team decided to drop the idea of shooting that song entirely. As the hero and reigning heart-throb Shahrukh Khan said, 'Nobody wanted to go to Switzerland without Yash Chopra.'

THE DIASPORA FACTOR

The 1990s were a crucial period in modern India's economic journey. The country had been run as a socialist, centrally planned and heavily protected economy for four decades after its independence from British rule. But in 1991 the economy was liberalised, the entry of foreign products and investments was facilitated and the earning opportunities for a vast number of Indians increased dramatically. With the easing of regulations, expensive multiplex cinemas with vastly improved facilities came to Indian cities, attracting an upmarket audience. The internet, satellite TV and mobile phones started ushering in a new visual culture, new aspirations and a sense of being connected to a global Indian presence. The possibilities of emergent middle classes travelling abroad for leisure increased. Meanwhile, a significant overseas Indian audience hungry for Indian movies had grown, and filmmakers started realising its economic potential.

As a result, the big movies of the 1990s were expensive, glossy productions and foregrounded Indian characters who lived and worked in places like London, New York or Melbourne, with designer clothes and glamorous lifestyles, even as the storylines glorified conservative social

values and played to the nostalgia of the non-resident Indian.

In 1995 Yash Chopra's son Aditya made one of the most successful and longest-running Hindi movies, *Dilwale Dulhaniya Le Jayenge* ('The Big-Hearted Will Whisk Away the Bride'). Astonishingly, this movie was shown daily for twenty-five years at Mumbai's Maratha Mandir theatre until the 2020 COVID-19 pandemic forced the cinema to close its doors. In the film, lead pair Kajol and Shahrukh Khan are London-based youngsters. The heroine's tradition-alist father has arranged her marriage with his friend's son back in India. She begs her father with folded hands to let her 'live' just once before she is married off and allow her to go on an Interrail tour of Europe with her friends. This sets the stage for the pair to meet and fall in love in countries across Europe – including Switzerland, of course. (Kajol and Khan are perhaps the most-loved pair in Indian screen history, and their life-size cut-outs can be found on Switzerland's Mount Titlis, where Indian tourists take mandatory selfies with their idols.)

The crux of the film is that the young hero follows the heroine to India but refuses to elope with her, as countless film couples had done earlier. He insists that he will win her father's heart and his consent for their marriage. This excessive veneration of family elders and the silencing of women's choices in the name of family honour were much celebrated as core Indian values by urban Indians as well as a huge nostalgic diasporic Indian market.

In director Karan Johar's blockbuster *Kabhi Khushi Kabhie Gham ...* ('Sometimes Happiness, Sometimes Sorrow', 2001) the hero lives in London. At a school function,

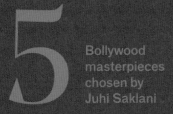

5

Bollywood
masterpieces
chosen by
Juhi Saklani

Guru Dutt
Pyaasa ('Thirsty')
1957

Sensitive and poor, poet Vijay finds that
the world only worships success. When
Vijay is presumed dead, Gulab, a prostitute
who loves him, sacrifices all she has to get
his work published. The poems are a hit,
and everyone who had mocked him now
claims him as their own. With superlative
songs and cinematography, auteur/actor
Guru Dutt's searing critique is routinely
found on all-time-great film lists.

Ramesh Sippy
Sholay ('Flames')
1975

India's wildly successful take on the spaghetti-
western genre, Sholay mixes outlaws,
horses and rugged terrain with humour,
sentiment and song-and-dance. Two brave
thugs are hired by a retired policeman to
capture a dreaded bandit alive. Slowly the
friends become emotionally invested in their
mission. The film ran at the Mumbai Minerva
theatre for five years, and its dialogues
are still remembered. Director Shekhar
Kapoor said that 'Indian film history can be
divided into Sholay BC and Sholay AD'.

Kundan Shah
Jaane Bhi Do Yaaro ('Who Pays the Piper')
1983

This heartbreaking, satirical tale lays bare
the corruption festering in the soul of a big
city like Bombay. Construction tycoons,
municipal authorities, police, media, social
workers ... all are components of a self-
serving system in which only the commoners
– personified by the two innocent and naive
heroes – are victimised. Yet the pitch-
perfect black humour, dialogue and acting
keep the audience laughing throughout.

Vishal Bharadwaj
Maqbool
2003

Shakespeare's Macbeth is beautifully
adapted to the context of 21st-century
Mumbai mafia, centring on a feared don,
his right-hand man – Maqbool – and the
don's mistress, passionately in love with
Maqbool, who inspires the don's murder.
Some of Hindi cinema's finest actors are
complemented by superb interpretations,
such as the witches of Macbeth being
reimagined as two corrupt policemen.

Anurag Kashyap
Gangs of Wasseypur (Parts 1 and 2)
2012

This epic tale of vengeance, hate, power and
politics spans three generations and takes
us inside the underdeveloped but coal-
rich mining belt of Jharkhand in northern
India. The film runs for 319 minutes and
was shown in two parts in India. It is an
opera of engaging characters, small-town
Indian politics, family sagas, wrenching
violence, earthy humour and unique music.

THE THREE KHANS

Aamir, Salman and Shah Rukh: three Indian Muslims who share the second name Khan, the year of their birth (1965) and the title 'King of Bollywood', a crown they have been contesting for three decades. Like Marvel superheroes, the three Khans dominate the Indian box office: they have starred in eight of the ten most successful Bollywood films of all time. There's no lack of rivalry between them: Shah Rukh Khan, or 'SRK', was on top in the 1990s and 2000s and introduced Bollywood to Western audiences with films like *Darr* ('Fear', 1993) and *Dilwale Dulhaniya le Jayenge* ('The Big-Hearted Will Whisk Away the Bride', 1995). For more than a decade now Aamir Khan has had the greatest global success – in 2016, *Dangal* ('Wrestling Competition'; see the article on Vinesh Phogat on page 163) became one of the fifteen most viewed films *ever* in China – while Salman Khan, the 'Bollywood Tiger', who is dogged by scandal (including being accused of hunting a protected species of antelope in Rajasthan), beats his rivals in terms of Indian audiences. In 2014, SRK was estimated to be the second-richest actor in the world, with a fortune of $600 million. Khan is a common name in Bollywood. The 'first Khan' is often considered to be Dilip Kumar (real name Muhammad Yusuf Khan), one of the biggest stars of the 1950s and 1960s and an early proponent of method acting. The less-contested title of 'fourth Khan' usually goes to Saif Ali Khan, star of the television series *Sacred Games*, the first big Netflix success in India. This has been compared with the American series *Narcos* because it tackles themes that Bollywood can't – or won't – confront, such as sex, politics and religion. Another contender for the title was Irrfan Khan, known in the West for his roles in *Slumdog Millionaire* and *Life of Pi*, who died aged just fifty-three in April 2020 after being diagnosed with a neuroendocrine tumour.

his son suddenly changes the plan of singing 'Do-Re-Mi' and leads a chorus of British children in singing the Indian national anthem instead. Moments such as these are tremendously emotional for Indians across the world, since they reverse a historic relationship of being colonised and considered inferior by Europeans. Successful heroes who hold their own in the West make the audience feel personally proud. (In *Kabhi Khushi Kabhie Gham* ... the family home of hero Shahrukh Khan is the palatial Waddesdon Manor in the UK, while the hero arrives home not in a car but by helicopter.)

In the 2000s film after film showed Indians living abroad: *Kal Ho Naa Ho* ('Tomorrow May Not Come', 2003: New York), *Salaam Namaste* (*Hello Greetings*, 2005: Melbourne), *Kabhi Alvida Naa Kehna* ('Never Say Goodbye', 2006: New York), *Namastey London* (2007: London), *Love Aaj Kal* (*Love Nowadays*, 2009: London and San Francisco), *Cocktail* (2012: London) and many more. Filmmakers were now able to bring more layers to their presentations of the foreign lands. Far from being idealised sites of dreams and honeymoons, in films like *Dil Chahta Hai* ('What the Heart Wants', 2001) and *Love Aaj Kal*, places like Sydney and San Francisco become locations where the Indian hero's successful but lonely and unhappy story unfolds.

GOOD FOR BUSINESS

It wasn't just mutual appreciation that had made the Swiss authorities honour Yash Chopra repeatedly. Thanks to his trendsetting films India emerged as the fourth-largest country of origin for tourists to Switzerland. Travel operators even offer guided tours of Swiss locations used in Bollywood scenes. Bollywood's role as a tourism-promotion strategy dawned on other countries as well – after all, the Indian film industry is one of the largest in the world, India is the second most populous country and its middle classes have shown a voracious appetite for holidaying abroad.

In 2011 *Zindagi Na Milegi Dobara* ('You Don't Live Twice') was produced in collaboration with the Spanish tourism promotion agency Turespaña. It showed us a bachelors' holiday of three friends having adventures across the beaches, cities and festival hotspots of Spain. The following year 60,444 Indians visited Spain, almost double the number from the previous year. Similarly, the spectacular shots of Iceland in the big-ticket production *Dilwale* ('The Big-Hearted', 2015) put the country on the imaginative map of Indians, and a flow of tourists began. Israel's prime minister, Benjamin Netanyahu, visited Mumbai himself in 2018 and met the leading figures in the industry in an event called Shalom Bollywood, inviting them to shoot in Israel.

Tourism apart, Bollywood is a business opportunity for smaller countries. At business conclaves of the Indian film industry, countries such as Kenya, Portugal, Malta, Jordan, Romania, Cyprus ... all compete for Bollywood business. They offer tax rebates to shoot, which increase if you hire local crew; some governments may even offer to co-fund the film.

For the filmmakers, on the other hand, foreign shooting has some unexpected benefits. India's notorious culture of complicated permissions, paperwork and bribery is absent, and there are no star-struck crowds to manage during the shoot.

THE PASSENGER   Juhi Saklani

Left: Set of the action film
Mumbai Saga in an Iranian café
in Mumbai. The film focuses on
the development of the city in the
1980s and 1990s.

and Amsterdam, initially frightened and lonely but gradually gaining friends, confidence and knowledge about the world – and herself.

In *English Vinglish* (2012), the late Sridevi plays an average Indian wife and mother whose family casually disrespect her because she cannot speak English and is not cosmopolitan in her behaviour. Visiting her sister in New York she secretly enrols in English classes – a multi-cultural world of their own – and these become her journey towards a self-respecting, autonomous self. With such cinema it would seem that Bollywood may be finally coming to terms with the 'foreign' and making it its own. ✎

Producers say they find stars easier to handle when they are not distracted by having to return home at night and without their friends and family around. Moreover, as an executive for Dharma Productions, one of Bollywood's leading production companies, said in an interview, 'Sometimes if you need to blow up cars, we don't have the highways to do it!'

Switzerland continues to thrive in this broader picture. In 2017 the tourism authorities hired Bollywood heart-throb Ranveer Singh as the brand ambassador for Switzerland Tourism in a bid to attract youngsters for adventure activities. They confidently predicted an increase in Indian footfall by as much as 25 per cent.

AND THE STORY CONTINUES …

In the decade starting 2010 two pioneering films successfully used foreign locations as an intrinsic part of their stories about Indian women – the movies had no leading men! Unlike Bollywood's earlier foreign excursions, these heroines were neither very rich nor romantic and not globetrotting holiday-makers either.

Queen (2013) shows us Kangana Ranaut as a young girl from Delhi, rejected by her fiancé for being unsophisticated, obstinately venturing on her planned honeymoon alone. The old 'honeymoon' shoot was thus completely subverted and reinvented as the clueless heroine negotiates Paris

The Blood of Tulips

Kashmiri writer Mirza Waheed explains
what it is to grow up in the world's most
militarised region, sandwiched between
India and Pakistan, where for decades the
desire for independence from India has been
met with fierce and unrelenting repression.

MIRZA WAHEED

Left: Amber Fort, near Jaipur,
Rajasthan.

There's a tulip garden in Kashmir. Spread over nearly thirty acres of magnificent terraces, it's girdled by the Zabarwan Hills at the back and overlooks the world-famous Dal Lake at the front. The garden is believed to be one of the largest in the world.

Every spring we have a government-run festival here to mark the beginning of the tourist season, during which tourists, residents and, on occasion, Indian soldiers, pose for photos amid a sea of red and yellow flowers. Colourful balloons soar into the sky, folk-music ensembles play string music, conflict-weary press photographers click away at the stunning vistas in the hope they'll get to send images of pretty flowers into the world instead of their usual fare: stills of young corpses and funeral marches.

Every year stories about the majestic tulip garden of Kashmir appear in the Indian and local press. Feature writers write eloquently about the breath of fresh air that the gardens bestow on the conflict-torn region; television crews make slick features, showing us clipped vox pops of selfie-driven tourists, local floriculturists and, of course, politicians hungry for photo ops.

I've been reading the same tulip story for at least ten years, and I have learned many things in the process. There are hundreds of thousands of bulbs planted across swathes of prime floral estate. Tulips usually bloom here in a four-week period from mid- or late March. The London-based World Book of Records has included the garden in its pages for a record of 1.2 million bulbs in 2017. It's been judged among the top five tulip gardens in the world by the World Tulip Summit Society in Canada. Last year it was reported that the garden created another world record for the highest number of blooms in the world – more than a million blooms of seventy varieties. Bollywood crews sometimes take over to film otherworldly song-and-dance sequences. Music videos are shot here – and why not?

Local people participate in large numbers, too, some for a brief respite from all the suffering and some in the hope of a bountiful tourist season. Others are there in the hope that the breathtaking garden might keep at bay memories of a lost loved one, even if momentarily, even if painfully.

If the winter lingers a bit too long, threatening to thwart the bloom, the authorities use high-tech polyhouses to help the tulips flower even in harsh conditions. The garden is also Wi-Fi enabled.

The same story, year after year, in journal after journal, on screen after screen. It doesn't matter what else is happening in that blighted land. The whole place might be oozing blood, under siege, the streets deserted, people cooped up inside their homes, weighed down by worries of dwindling food and medicine, but at least we have a successful tulip festival. The tulips and the attendant pageantry paint a beautifully rosy picture of Kashmir, a rare warm and fuzzy moment in an otherwise mournful place, wracked by conflict for more than three decades.

The long war in and over Kashmir began soon after the decolonisation of

MIRZA WAHEED is a writer and journalist originally from Kashmir and now based in the UK. He is the author of *The Collaborator* (Penguin, 2011), which was shortlisted for the Guardian First Book Award, *The Book of Gold Leaves* (Penguin, 2014) and *Tell Her Everything* (Westland, 2018). All his novels are set, at least in part, against the backdrop of Kashmir and the ongoing tension between India and Pakistan.

'After the turn of the millennium, as the insurgency diminished significantly, Kashmiris decided to take to the streets in their hundreds of thousands.'

South Asia in 1947. At the time, Kashmir, an independent state, was left undecided so that a referendum under the aegis of the United Nations could be held to allow Kashmiris a say in their destiny, whether to join India or Pakistan. The plebiscite never took place; instead, the two countries have since fought three wars over the region. Kashmiris, wounded by various betrayals by Delhi as it sought to manage Kashmir via servile unionists, decided to take up arms soon after the *annus horribilis* of 1987, when a state election was massively rigged to prevent a new and popular Kashmiri party from acquiring legislative power. Pakistan readily gave Kashmiris arms and training, resulting in a full-blown armed and mass movement in the early 1990s. Almost overnight Kashmir turned into a slaughterhouse. The conflict has continued to rage since then, with ebbs and flare-ups, killing at least seventy thousand people. After the turn of the millennium, as the insurgency diminished significantly, Kashmiris decided to take to the streets in their hundreds of thousands. Rivers of the young and old, men and women, on the streets every year. But India responded in the same manner as it had to the armed uprising, with limitless force: killing, maiming and blinding hundreds, including children.

*

For years I've looked at pictures of the red dazzle spread over the verdant land that borders the Dal Lake, favoured by imperial Mughals in the past and ministers, administrators and spooks in the present day. The

Governor House – the palatial home of the rulers that India sends to Kashmir from time to time – is close by, as are the state chief minister's residence and some other 'VIP' villas and chalets.

The arrogant efflorescence on display should make me feel happy, even proud. It's less than half an hour's drive from my parents' home in Srinagar, the largest city in Kashmir. It should perhaps even make me feel a bit patriotic about our fertile soil and luminous vegetation. I should celebrate it as many people do. At least Kashmir is in the news for happier, more colourful reasons.

Positive news, you see, has been in such short supply during Kashmir's many seasons of blood-letting that we must paint the internet red with Kashmiri tulips. And truly, when in full blossom, the garden does look like something quite out of this world, like the masterwork of a *rangrez*, as if a possessed dyer has been at work all night, as if someone has unfurled a vast red-velvet carpet over the bowl of the valley.

Like most people, I love flowers. I grew my own when I was a child in Kashmir: pansies, roses, hyacinths and irises. And the sight of the garden does please the senses enormously. But each time I see the pictures it also makes me feel a bit unsettled, uneasy, perhaps even guilty.

In moments of epistemic despair, I imagine the blood of Kashmir's countless dead trickling down from the hills, the gorges, the gardens and the graveyards in the countryside and issuing forth in an insanely beautiful display in the prime real estate of the city where some of our ruling elites prefer to live.

*

When I was in Kashmir recently, I walked past the garden and its splendid surroundings. I saw it in its bare, unflowered state. Perhaps because it wasn't the season for mesmerising flower carpets, I realised that a dreaded torture centre – Papa II – is close to the tulip garden named after the late Indian prime minister Indira Gandhi. The building was whitewashed, literally and metaphorically, a few years after it was decommissioned in 1996 as a place where Indian soldiers used to put live electric wires to the genitals of illegally detained young boys. Many boys never returned from there, and those who did were impaired for life. The colonial-era structure, previously a guesthouse called The Fairview, was turned into an official residence in the late 1990s after local bureaucrats had it exorcised (you read that right), probably owing to some confused moral residue or perhaps because they were superstitious enough to believe that the ghosts of those who were tormented inside might come back to revisit. More recently Papa II served as the official residence of Kashmir's last chief minister. In a place where no one has ever been prosecuted for war crimes, it's probably fitting that a ruler found safety and comfort within a torture chamber.

I asked a Kashmiri writer and journalist why every media outlet wants a tulip piece or other stories of that nature from Kashmir. I understand the journalistic impulse and duty to cover it, and it should

Indo-Pakistani Conflicts

1947 August
End of British rule. The subcontinent is divided on the basis of religion into India and Pakistan (the latter is in turn divided into East and West Pakistan). Mass migration causes violence between Hindus, Muslims and Sikhs: hundreds of thousands of people die, leading to an atmosphere of hostility that lasts for decades. The regions of Jammu and Kashmir are claimed by both new countries.

1947–9 October–January
After an invasion by tribal militias armed by Pakistan in an uprising against the maharajah of Kashmir, military assistance is sought from India, resulting in Kashmir acceding to India in October 1947 ahead of the planned UN-madated plebiscite to determine its future. The First Indo-Pakistani War ends with Kashmir divided into two territories, one controlled by India and the other by Pakistan, demarcated by the Ceasefire Line (since 1972 known as the Line of Control).

1965 August
Following attempts by the Pakistani military to provoke an uprising against India in Kashmir (Operation Gibraltar), the Second Indo-Pakistani War breaks out. Five weeks of hostilities end thanks to United Nations intervention. The two sides sign a peace agreement, the Tashkent Declaration, in January 1966.

1971 December
The Third Indo-Pakistani War is the biggest and bloodiest of the three and doesn't take place in Kashmir but in East Pakistan, where a civil war is brought to an end with the support of the Indian Army. East Pakistan gains independence and takes the name Bangladesh. During

be written about, but why the relentless focus every summer? He said it's rather simple to grasp. Editors sometimes turn down the familiar death-and-devastation journalism from Kashmir and want an uplifting story instead. As reporters file stories and pictures of shootings, massacres, blindings, nocturnal raids, torture, extra-judicial killings, houses blown up by Indian forces, militant attacks, assassinations – because that's what they've had to focus on all their lives – inured to the endless suffering of Kashmir, they want pretty pictures instead. It's too depressing. Surely, life must go on. Where are the beautiful houseboats and flower-laden shikaras? The colours of spring, normality, peace, tourist season, even when they don't exist or are as short lived as the flight of a bullet, need some focus, too, you know. It suits the state as well, both the central command in Delhi and their representatives in Kashmir. Let's not forever harp on the tragic conflict of Kashmir. The world must know the place also has a garden that people pay to see in spring ... In its belligerent quest for a narrative shift on Kashmir, the Indian state deploys everything in its arsenal to declare peace has arrived. Year after year. But then, as Tacitus would say, 'they make a desolation and call it peace'.

Because – as we read about the record number of tulips every year, the ticket sales to the garden, the annual inauguration by successive client elites, the chief ministers and assorted chief guests – other numbers,

the brief but violent conflict, millions of East Pakistanis take refuge in India.

1974 *May* India successfully tests its first nuclear weapon near its border with Pakistan (Operation Smiling Buddha).

1989 *July* After the contested elections of 1987, a mass uprising against Indian rule (still ongoing) erupts in Kashmir. Some insurgents seek independence while others want to join Pakistan, which supports the uprising that over the years has shifted from being a nationalistic and secularist movement to an Islamic one.

1998 *May* Pakistan conducts six nuclear tests. After being condemned by the international community, India adopts a No First Use (NFU) policy to which it still adheres:

the use of nuclear weapons is permitted only in response to a nuclear attack.

1999 *May–July* India launches aerial strikes against forces supported by Pakistan that have invaded Indian Kashmir in the conflict known as the Kargil War. International diplomacy convinces Pakistan to pull back to its established borders.

2008 *November* Ten Pakistanis associated with the terrorist group Lashkar-e-Taiba attack buildings in Mumbai, killing 164 people.

2019 *February* A suicide attack in Indian Kashmir by the terrorist group Jaish-e-Mohammed kills more than forty Indian paramilitary personnel. Delhi responds with aerial strikes on the other side of the Line of Control.

other gardens, other flowers hover darkly.

Away from the sanitised, militarised tourist district – where a postcard-pretty eighteen-hole golf course, the ghastly torture house and paramilitary camps flank the tulip field – close to people's homes in the old city lies another vast garden: the Eidgah of Srinagar. It's mostly a plain field, dusty, without manicured landscaping or a ticket booth.

During my childhood all of it used be a vast open prayer ground, filling up with thousands of worshippers every Eid. A sea of white caps one moment, an iridescent wave of prostrate forms the next. Soon, however, as the war broke out in 1989 it began to be filled up with our dead. Kashmiris had risen up in arms. They went to Pakistan-administered Kashmir where Pakistani agencies gave them weapons. They shouted '*Azadi!*' (freedom) on every street, every day and every night, I remember, demanding their right to self-determination, a promise India's first prime minister, Jawaharlal Nehru, made to them soon after India and Pakistan became independent.

The Indian state responded with a ruthlessness reminiscent of that of Colonel Reginald Dyer at Jallianwala Bagh, Amritsar, in 1919 (the infamous massacre when the British officer ordered his troops to gun down hundreds of unarmed Indian protestors who had gathered in a walled garden), killing thousands, civilians and militants alike. A part of the prayer ground was then quickly designated as the 'martyrs' graveyard', a final resting place for those shot dead by the Indian armed forces and police. It expanded fast, as the number of stone and marble gravestones bearing Urdu and Persian couplets and, of course, verses from the Qur'an, grew week after week. Tended with the delicate care and love of the broken hearted, graveyard irises

AN ARBITRARY LINE

The Second World War coincided with the culmination of Indian independence movements, such as the one led by Gandhi, and the UK, deeply in debt after the war, didn't have the resources to maintain its control of the subcontinent. Thus began the decolonisation of India, a process that, according to British officials, should have taken five years but had to be condensed into four months. The division of the territory into two independent nations, one Muslim (Pakistan – East, now Bangladesh, and West, now Pakistan) and the other officially secular with a majority of Hindus (India), needed to be done as fast as possible. Enter Sir Cyril Radcliffe, a lawyer from London recruited to establish a line between the two countries. Sir Cyril had never been to India, was unfamiliar with its politics and society and arrived there shortly before the British left. He spent

(*mazar munje* in Kashmiri) prospered in the fertile ground. Soon, rose stalks leaned by the side of the dark headstones.

In another part of town, the *sang-tarash*, traditional stonemasons, worked into the night with their chisels to create elegant memorial tablets for the new garden in the middle of the city. By the mid-1990s the freshly sprouted cemetery teemed with row upon row of tombstones of the young and old, of those killed by the soldiers but also of those killed by the insurgents. A necropolis was born where kites used to fly in the spring only a few years ago.

Kashmiris grow flowers here, too, hallowed ground as it is for them. They come here on Eid, on Fridays or any time the heart can't bear the separation any more, to offer prayers, to converse with their slain kin. Outside the graveyard, in the greater part of the prayer ground as yet not given over to the dead, children play cricket, jostle and banter like I used to as a teenager, a time when there were neither fresh graves here nor old tombs. Today, more than thirty years after the first bullet-ridden body was interred, many of the graves have flowers nodding next to them. In summer the graveyard, now fenced off to set it apart from the rest of the ground, shines all white and pink.

Some days, as you go past, you can discern a form bent over or sitting beside a tombstone. At the far, southern end of the vast ground I noticed that a children's play area has arrived, and if you walk along the entire length of the adjacent road – the Eidgah Road – you can see the playground, swings and slides, the martyrs' cemetery, the remainder of the old prayer ground and, lastly, an old mosque in an unbroken stretch. It's not very often you see such cradle-to-grave imagery in one place.

During the last three decades, similar graveyard-gardens of different sizes have

five weeks on the task. In India, Sikhs, Hindus, Muslims and Christians had always lived alongside one another, making any geographical division based on religion hugely problematic. Nevertheless, the lawyer analysed the districts in each state and 'allocated' those that were mainly Muslim to Pakistan and those that were mainly Hindu to India. What followed was one of the biggest mass migrations ever, characterised by extreme violence. Even today, the Radcliffe Line is a major presence in the lives of Indian, Pakistani and Bangladeshi people: its three thousand kilometres on the India–Pakistan border are heavily guarded and so highly illuminated as to be visible from space. The border has divided families and cuts through fields, forests and rivers. It also strikes through the pilgrimage route between the two most important sacred sites of Sikhism, the Golden Temple of Amritsar and the Gurdwara Darbar Sahib Kartarpur in Kartarpur, Pakistan.

(January 1989 –November 2019)

Total deaths	95,471
Deaths in state or police custody	7,135
Civilian arrests	158,339
Buildings burned or destroyed	109,450
Widowed women	22,910
Orphaned children	107,780
Women victims of gang-rape or molestation	11,175

SOURCE: KASHMIR MEDIA SERVICE

cropped up in other towns and villages in what was once an Edenic land, 'the paradise on earth', as the 13th-century mystic poet Amir Khusro described it. The living in Kashmir now keep their dead close by, as mnemonic totems of their lost ones but also as urgent reminders of who did this to them.

The year 2018 was Kashmir's most violent year in a decade or so. Nearly six hundred people were killed and some of the dead found their burial place in the Eidgah. It's a ritual that has been practised for over thirty years.

*

Further afield, in the lush countryside, there are more traditional gardens and grounds, signifiers of Kashmir's geography and culture: apple orchards, acres and acres of them, which for centuries have been a source of livelihood and dreams for many. It's in the environs of these orchards, in the midst of them, that some new corpses are found. South Kashmir, where orchards would throw up dead bodies even in the 1990s, and which has of late emerged as a hub for a new generation of militants and protestors, has witnessed dozens of encounters between the Indian armed forces and Kashmiri rebels in the last couple of years.

It is from this fiery cauldron that the suicide bomber Adil Dar – who carried out the devastating Pulwama attack in February 2019, killing forty-four Central Reserve Police Force troopers – came. As the Kashmiri journalist Basharat Peer writes, Dar didn't emerge from a vacuum. He was born and raised in south Kashmir on a diet of humiliation and indignity. Until things change, Kashmir will continue to produce young men with less of a fear of death than of living in a vast open-air prison.

Here fathers recognise the bodies of their teenage sons while attending to the wounded in a hospital. Here men are turned into human shields as Indian soldiers look for militants hiding in the orchards. Here the soldiers shoot young boys dead as they throw stones or raise slogans when they see their militant friends surrounded, or even if they're merely present near the site of an encounter. In recent years young Kashmiris, men and women, have flocked to battle sites in the countryside to save local boys who have

Right: Hamid Anwar, 76-year-old university professor and resident of Srinagar, at his daughter's home during a visit to Delhi.

The Blood of Tulips

picked up guns to fight Indian rule. These are ordinary young Kashmiris who fully recognise it's akin to staring death in the face, but they do it nonetheless because they've lost all hope and all fear.

Of the eleven people killed on 15 December 2018 after an encounter in the Pulwama district, around forty kilometres from Srinagar, seven were civilians, three were militants and one was a soldier. An eyewitness said, 'The forces could've left the spot easily. But they fired to kill.' Among those killed was year-twelve student Shahnawaz. His father, Muhammad Yusuf, had this to say: 'The encounter had ended and [the] forces were moving out when my son went out to fetch a bucket of water from a spring across the road. There were protests going on in nearby villages. He was on his way back when forces fired directly at him from inside the vehicle ... I watched him fall down as he cried for help. They killed him in front of my eyes, and I watched it all helplessly.'

I read and saw interviews with the parents of the slaughtered boys, and each one of them signed off on a note of ultimate despair and defiance: 'Why don't they kill us all ... ? We want the army to leave. We want freedom ...'

Less than a week before the massacre in Pulwama two teenage militants, one fourteen and the other seventeen, were killed in an encounter outside Srinagar. What catastrophe, what injustice, did the two friends witness to make them abandon their school textbooks in favour of a rifle, knowing full well they wouldn't last long against one of the largest armies in the world?

The scroll of the dead rolls on and in columns from month to month, year to year, going back to the late 1980s. The year 2018 was the deadliest in a decade. But then again, which year in Kashmir's modern history hasn't been a year of the dead?

I was a teenager when we started the death count. Now, at more than seventy thousand, we are into a second- and third-generation catalogue of death. In some years only a hundred-odd are killed, in other years and other seasons more than five hundred. The great Kashmiri-American poet Agha Shahid Ali once wrote about 'Freedom's terrible thirst, flooding Kashmir ...' And the flood continues unabated, with blood given by everyone: civilians, militants, policemen, Indian soldiers stationed to keep Kashmir under Indian rule and, most precious of all, the children of Kashmir. Since 2010 Indian paramilitaries and police have used buckshot to stymie civilian protests in Kashmir. These Victorian-era weapons, originally designed to hunt birds in flight, spray hundreds of tiny lead pellets, often catching people in their faces and eyes.

All this blood, all the killing, all the brutality we saw over the past decades ... curls back in different threads to the existential question that Kashmiris have posed for ever: the question of their future. It also reinforces in unambiguous terms the image of India in the minds of Kashmiris as an armed aggressor, as an occupying military power.

I was only a boy when I looked at the banal aftermath of one of the most barbaric massacres in Kashmir: a doleful mound of abandoned slippers on a street not far from my ancestral home in Srinagar. The people who had been wearing them until the day before were probably already recumbent in morgues and graveyards. 'Bullets rained in all directions and [the] dead fell like the apples fall from the trees when they are ripe,' recalls survivor Nazir Baba.

More than fifty mourners, including four women, were killed in the Hawal massacre of 21 May 1990, when Indian paramilitaries showered bullets at the funeral procession of Kashmir's chief cleric, Mirwaiz Farooq, who'd been assassinated by militants earlier that day. A survivor remembers seeing the paramilitaries frisking the dead, snatching earrings and pendants from the dead women. This was a time when we used to witness or hear the sounds of a massacre as though they'd always been an integral part of life.

What's new, however, is the death-defying fearlessness of a new generation of Kashmiris who rush towards an encounter to create a distraction, an interlude, so the holed-up militant, who might be a friend, neighbour or kin, can escape. When I was growing up, the impulse and the rule was to run away from an encounter site not towards it.

In 2018 Kashmir saw more than a hundred such encounters, and the standard operating procedure for Indian forces seems to have been to kill anyone in their crosshairs. Anyone. As a result, of the more than five hundred casualties that year, 160 were civilians, including thirty-one children and eighteen women. Also in 2018, hundreds were injured and at least forty shot in their eyes, including twenty-month-old baby Hiba, whose vision in her right eye, doctors say, may never return.

*

But what happened, what was done, in 2018 is even starker than the explosive summer of 2016, the year of mass blinding in Kashmir. Following the killing of a popular militant leader, more than a thousand young people were shot with buckshot pellets, causing serious injuries to their eyes and blinding more than a hundred. These are children, blinded for life, who would never see the tulips.

Away from the flower shows, the collective punishment of Kashmiris continues

ARTICLE 370

Kashmir has been administered by India since 1947 but gained a certain level of independence in 1949 with the establishment of Article 370 of the Indian Constitution. This gave it a special status, with its own prime minister, flag and legislative assembly, while India would still control its foreign affairs, defence and communications. Any law made in India has to be approved by Kashmir before it can come into force there. At least, that was the case until August 2019, when Article 370 was abolished by presidential decree and Modi's government launched a campaign of military repression, arresting local leaders and isolating people by imposing a communications blackout and a curfew. Article 370 restricted access to university places and some forms of state employment to residents of Kashmir. By abolishing Article 370 and also Article 35A, which stated that only Kashmiris could own land in the state, Delhi has opened up the way for Indian citizens to invest and settle in Kashmir. The Indian-administered region was also divided into two federal territories: Jammu and Kashmir; and Ladakh. Officially this was done for security reasons and to promote economic development, but, in fact, it was a way of increasing Indian control. Indian Kashmir has a majority-Muslim population, but even the mainly Hindu and largely BJP-voting population of Jammu feels betrayed by Modi's actions. The revoking of Article 370 has also made Muslims all over India feel increasingly under threat.

unchecked – or, perhaps it should be said, with renewed force – under the new regime in India. The spooks and generals in Delhi, who essentially run Kashmir for India, have, in fact, called it exactly that: Operation All-Out. On the ground and in people's homes in Kashmir, it's translated into large-scale violence against civilians, the nightly raids on people's homes, the slapping of draconian laws on anyone who dares to resist, the burning and destruction of family homes of insurgents or of homes where militants might have spent a night, detention of family members, the humiliations and arrests of teenage stone throwers.

The state government in Kashmir is run by unionists who take turns to be the intermediaries of Delhi – until they are summarily cast off in favour of a man from Delhi. Displaying great moral dexterity, they trade blame as each set sits in the seat of cosmetic power or its opposition. When in power they order inquiries into the killings that are almost always buried in the black hole of dark laws that provide immunity to Indian forces and the police; when not in power they issue profoundly sorrowful sound bites and accuse their in-power opponents of callousness.

In J.M. Coetzee's novel *Waiting for the Barbarians* (Penguin USA, 2010/Vintage UK, 2004) the magistrate who runs the frontier settlement and who's shaken by the torture of nomadic 'barbarians', remarks: 'The Empire does not require that its servants love each other, merely that they perform their duty.' Kashmir will continue to see killings, plunder and the trading of place and blame. Office bearers from the ruling 'elites' in Kashmir will take turns to express grief at blood spilled by an apparatus of which they are a small but essential cog – 'the teeth of the axe', as the Kashmiri proverb goes. As Coetzee's

magistrate returns the tortured nomadic girl to her people, he speaks of himself as 'a jackal of empire in sheep's clothing'.

The new statistics will simply add to the rolling journal of death that Kashmiris keep in their hearts and minds. They will add it to the at least eight thousand people forcibly disappeared over the years and with at least seven thousand of those buried in unmarked graves in the mountains. Or with those who carry the deep scars of oppression on their bodies and minds. Since 1989 one in every six Kashmiris may have faced some form of torture; that's almost one from every other family. In 2016, in the first detailed report into the mental-health situation in Kashmir, Médecins Sans Frontières revealed that nearly 50 per cent of the population suffer from some form of PTSD. Half the population.

But we must, of course, also look at the number of tourists who visit the gardens of Kashmir.

*

Mostly ignored by the international powers as they seek to curry favour with the growing market in India, Kashmir today is entirely in the grip of a monstrous campaign of suppression by the Indian state. No one gives a damn really. Until recently one used to take heart from the token candlelight vigil in Delhi or elsewhere in solidarity with the coffin-bearers of Kashmir, but now, perhaps battered by far-right TV channels and the robot lobbies of troll farms, many in India appear to have pressed the mute button on Kashmir.

As the UN published its first ever exhaustive report into human-rights abuses in Indian-administered and Pakistan-administered Kashmir, the Indian state dismissed it as fallacious. Influential media bosses and journalists, rather than

THE SEVEN SISTERS

Kashmir isn't the only Indian-administered region to be affected by independence movements. There has always been strong separatist feeling in the seven states of the extreme north-east, the so-called seven sisters of Arunachal Pradesh, Assam, Manipur, Meghalaya, Mizoram, Nagaland and Tripura. These are joined to the rest of the country only by the narrow Siliguri Corridor between Nepal and Bangladesh and are home to tribal populations, some of which have been in conflict with the Indian state ever since its inception. The Nagas, for example, fought fiercely for independence and for their tribe to be united rather than being scattered throughout Manipur, Assam and Arunachal Pradesh. This struggle resulted in the creation of Nagaland in 1963. But each time one Naga group has signed an accord with the central government, as with the ceasefire in 1975, old and new separatist groups have continued their guerrilla activities in pursuit of complete independence rather than settling for a shared territory with other Nagas. The situation in the multi-ethnic state of Manipur is more complex still. There, various tribal groups, including the Kukis, Meiteis, Nagas and Pangals, are fighting for autonomy and recognition of their distinct culture. India has responded to the separatist threat with an iron fist and by applying the highly controversial Armed Forces Special Powers Act (AFSPA), which grants the Indian Army immunity in dealing with the situation. In protest against the many massacres in Manipur whose perpetrators have never been brought to justice, the activist Irom Sharmila undertook the longest hunger strike ever recorded, from 2000 to 2016, becoming the figurehead of widespread opposition to the AFSPA.

'On 5 August 2019 India erased the long-held autonomy of Kashmir by unilaterally revoking Article 370 of the Indian Constitution, which guaranteed Kashmir's special status.'

looking into the report and asking questions of the state – doing their job, in fact – decided it was best to ignore it or, better still, dismiss it as unfounded. It was an exhaustive, well-substantiated investigation that detailed endemic abuse.

What does all this mean? An almost total suspension of normal legal and moral systems when it comes to Kashmir. Such has been the viciousness of India's recent operations that even the most heart-rending stories are pushed off the radar in no time. In autumn 2019 a young bag-maker from Srinagar was shot dead as he came out of his house to check on a noise. As outraged residents took to the streets, first in protest then as part of his funeral march, the paramilitaries and police charged at them with tear gas and pellet guns. The young man's friend and neighbour, utterly bereft at not being allowed to mourn his benefactor, his shirt torn as he howled in the middle of a street, then pleaded with the armed forces to kill him, too.

In 2017, in another illustration of how far the Indian state has moved away from basic democratic norms and the rule of law, the army chief gave a medal of commendation to a torture-loving major who tied a Kashmiri shawl-weaver to the front of a pick-up truck and paraded him for six hours. Something terrible has been unleashed at the heart of the new Indian state. Edward Said once wrote about the 'uncompromising brutality against the latest bunch of "natives"' and of the 'reductive polarisations' of conflict in the modern world. Said also emphasised the urgency of a humanism gone out of fashion among postmodern elites. While he expressly renews his advocacy for Palestinian self-determination, Said makes sure it's at a remove from the 'mutual hostility' that has prevailed in the Middle East and elsewhere. Increasingly in India, owing to a terrifying rise in right-wing majoritarianism and a hardening of attitudes among the middle classes, the basic dignity due to an oppressed people, in Kashmir and elsewhere, has been significantly eroded or vanished altogether. The hostility now appears to be complete, unbridgeable and, for those on the receiving end, unbearable.

*

On 5 August 2019 India erased the long-held autonomy of Kashmir by unilaterally revoking Article 370 of the Indian Constitution, which guaranteed Kashmir's special status within the larger Indian union pending a final resolution of one of the longest-running conflicts in the world. Since then nearly eight million Kashmiris have been living under a punishing crackdown imposed by the Indian government. For weeks the region was cut off from the rest of the world, as the Indian state cut off the internet, mobile phones, even old-fashioned landlines. People were not allowed to assemble let alone protest, schools and offices were shut, healthcare services deteriorated dramatically as patients couldn't call their doctors or ambulances, word of the death of one's kin reached people days after funerals had taken place. All this, while thousands of ordinary people, including politicians of all hues, activists, lawyers, business leaders, essentially anyone with a modicum of influence, but, most worryingly, children as young as nine, were thrown into prison. The BBC and *The New York Times* and fact-finding missions by some Indian activists have turned up evidence of torture, denial of justice as law courts remain inactive and an overall unprecedented suspension of basic civil liberties. While some mobile-phone services were restored after nearly two months, internet provision is restricted to 2G and text messages are barred. Schools and businesses remain shut as Kashmiris have launched a quiet civil-disobedience movement by refusing to partake in a narrative of normality that the Indian state has tried to manufacture. One BBC report noted that Kashmir's economy had suffered losses to the tune of more than one billion dollars since August 2019. By all accounts and from my conversations with people at 'home' in Kashmir, it is a siege like no other: a medieval siege of blockade and mass incarceration and a modern, technological one in which people are deprived of their voices, as rudimentary tools of both analogue and digital communication are suspended.

In 2018, the thirtieth year of blood in Kashmir, we saw yet another carnival of blood: we saw parents plead with their militant kids to return home, and we saw a father behold the face of his slain teenage son who perhaps understood, or perhaps he didn't, the might of the country he chose to fight against.

But, above all, we saw India come down on the people of Kashmir with a punitive wrath that harks back to the darkest of times, the early 1990s, when Indian armed forces committed massacre after massacre, burned down entire localities, killed, raped, detained and tortured hundreds. The kin of the slain, stunned into silence or thrown into paroxysms of grief at the sight of a shattered body, create real and imagined memorials to cling on to. They create rooms, they preserve memorabilia, they offer flowers on fresh graves.

All of it joins up to form a long, forever-ringing arc of sadness and despair. Every bullet, every death, every howl, through years and decades of Kashmir's solitary, cold suffering. For years now, for long decades now (with profound apologies to Agha Shahid), death has 'turned every day in Kashmir into some family's Karbala'.

Kashmir today, then, is Karbala more than ever. In its grief, in its vast tragedy and in its lonely but resolute defiance. But when the houses are burned, when the children are slaughtered or their eyes stolen, Kashmir will still remain.

We will grow flowers, dazzling tulips and graveyard irises, we will make our houseboats pretty, we will decorate our guesthouses by the lake or in the hills, we will cook wazwan, we will take exams, publish newspapers, write poetry and code, run businesses, and we will lift ourselves up in a cycle of hope and despair ... Because that child's got to be given *batte,* food, in faith that she will live to see a fresh dawn but sometimes also in fear that she, too, might transform into blood, like the fourteen-year-old boy whose perforated body his mother saw one month and his matriculation exam certificate the next.

When I wrote this, Kashmir was emerging from the grip of a long Himalayan winter, a season when Kashmiris try to soothe their new and old scars with warmth and dark humour. In spring they begin a fresh year in their long struggle for dignity and freedom; they will hope the world will at last take proper notice of them, as it does of the arresting beauty of their homeland.

As for me, I will return home again and hope to look at the gorgeous flowers, but I will know that there is a dark river that lies beneath. 🖋

In the Ring with India's Most Powerful Woman

Wrestling had always been a male sport in India until Vinesh Phogat and her cousins came along. Now she out-earns most of her male colleagues and dreams of Olympic gold.

SONIA FALEIRO

Left: Two athletes during freestyle wrestling practice at the Sir Chhotu Ram Stadium in Rohtak, Haryana.

One brisk evening in January 2019 several thousand people, warmly dressed in jumpers and scarves, took their seats in a stadium on the outskirts of Delhi for the latest round of India's Pro Wrestling League. The PWL is to wrestling what the Indian Premier League is to cricket: a jamboree of international athletes, bright lights and big money. Of all the wrestling stars out that night, one shone more brightly than the rest. At 8 p.m. the announcer's voice came through the speaker system to whip the crowd up for the next bout. Then, with the athletes ready backstage, he roared her name: 'Viiiiinesh Phoooooogaaaaat!!!' Vinesh Phogat, a tiny woman in her mid-twenties with delicate features, perfect teeth and muscles as round and taut as fresh oranges, emerged from the tunnel in a red cape and strode towards the wrestling mat through an avenue of flames.

Phogat is one of the world's leading freestyle wrestlers. She won her first gold medal at the Commonwealth Games in 2014, followed by another in 2018. Four months later she became the first Indian woman to win a wrestling gold at the Asian Games. Phogat comes from a family of wrestlers: two of her cousins have won Commonwealth golds, and her husband, Somvir Rathee, is also a professional wrestler. But, although her cousins have been derailed by fame or injury, Phogat continues her climb to the pinnacle of the sport. She remains an odds-on favourite to make the podium at the next Olympics.

In wrestling you score points by pinning your opponent to the mat. During the three bouts that Phogat had fought in this year's league so far, she had conceded just three points and won twenty-eight. Her opponent that night, another Indian called Seema, was the underdog. The wrestlers took up their starting positions on the mat, crouching low with their arms entwined and foreheads touching. For several seconds they were locked in this position, feeling for any loss of poise in their opponent that might give them an opportunity to take them down. Then suddenly Phogat pulled on Seema's arms, knocked her off balance, and lunged at her like a cheetah attacking a stumbling gazelle.

On the mat the cheetah became a boa constrictor. Phogat wrapped her opponent in her arms and legs, locking her there and squeezing the fight out of her. An apparently vulnerable position can be reversed quickly with a sudden surge of energy. With Seema trying to tug her down to the floor, Phogat ducked under her opponent's outstretched arms to seize her around the

SONIA FALEIRO is the author of *The Good Girls: An Ordinary Killing* (Grove Atlantic USA/ Bloomsbury UK/Penguin India, 2021), which investigates the hanging of two teenagers in a village in India. Her previous book, *Beautiful Thing: Inside the Secret World of Bombay's Dance Bars* (Grove Atlantic USA/Canongate UK/Penguin India, 2011) was named a book of the year by the *Guardian*, the *Observer*, *The Sunday Times*, *The Economist* and *Time Out*. She is a co-founder of Deca, a cooperative of award-winning writers. She lives in London.

'When Phogat is not wrestling she can be a picture of charm ... but in training or during matches she is cold, hard and quickly angered by any sign of disrespect.'

waist. Then, bending her knees low to get her weight under her opponent, Phogat rolled backwards and flipped Seema over her shoulder. In the audience, plump dignitaries in bright-orange turbans sat comfortably on white-leather armchairs, discoursing on the spectacle. Soon Phogat was leading 6-0.

Phogat's success makes her a rarity twice over. Wrestling is hugely popular in India. Millions tune in to watch live bouts on TV, but the vast majority of fighters are men. The average Indian woman makes less than 200 rupees ($2.80) an hour. Yet, as a star wrestler – and one of the few females in the sport – Phogat earned around $35,000 for five matches at the PWL, each lasting six minutes. Only one male wrestler earned more. In 2018 her total earnings from wrestling were around $500,000.

After the bout Phogat headed to the dugout where she slumped down on the ground, exhausted. She buried her face in her sweatshirt while her husband and her physiotherapist, Rucha Kashalkar, watched her warily. When Phogat is not wrestling she can be a picture of charm, with a politician's flair for making someone she meets feel like they are the most important person in the room. But in training or during matches she is cold, hard and quickly angered by any sign of disrespect.

As she wound down, her fans began to inch closer to the dugout, leaning over its edge to snap selfies with her. Phogat mostly ignored them, but at one point a pushy man with a paunch thrust his way forward with his young daughter. 'Autograph!' he shouted. 'Take a photo! Take a photo!'

'Vinesh!' the girl cried.

Her father gently corrected her, telling his daughter to address Phogat as 'Aunty'. Aunty is a common but complex term, used by Indian children when they talk to their friends' mothers or their mother's friends. But it can also imply that someone is frumpy or conservative; if used to address a famous or successful stranger it sounds condescending, as though you can be familiar with her just because she is a woman.

Phogat looked up. 'Aunty?' she snapped. She has feline eyes and a warm smile, but when she opens her mouth the voice you hear is deep and raw. She comes from the rural north-Indian state of Haryana, where the dialect consists of short, declarative sentences that shoot out like bullets.

'Well, you're married now,' the man cackled. 'So get used to being called an aunty.'

'This country is something else,' Phogat muttered as she turned away. Even with her face grey with exhaustion, her hair matted with sweat and her mouth hanging open as she cooled down, she was resolute and immovable. Phogat was no one's aunty.

Phogat was born in Balali, a four-hour drive north of central Delhi. One January morning in 2019 I drove to the village to meet her mother, Premlata Singh, who still lives there. The 52-year-old has a very different life from her neighbours. Balali is a typical village in these parts, made up of an orderly series of single-storey houses with mud walls and tin roofs on which residents store food for their animals, unused bicycles and other household items to make more space inside. Electricity is intermittent, and the main source of fuel is buffalo dung, the scent of which drifts through the air along with the tweets and chirrups of red-wattled lapwings. Women with veiled faces hurry around performing chores, and the men, their moustaches neatly curled, lounge on charpoys, tugging on bubbling hookahs and talking politics. 'They think being seen to work lowers their status,' a woman sneered as she balanced a basket of dung on her head. 'We look after the children, cook food, draw milk, wash the buffaloes and help with the harvest. We work, but they control the money.'

Farther into the village a mansion gleams like a moonstone from behind tall gates, its driveway furnished with a red SUV and patrolled by an Alsatian dog, a status symbol in this part of India. Phogat built this house for her mother, a Bollywood fantasy of the high life made real. Inside, a vast living room is furnished with ornately carved wooden furniture and vitrines full of Phogat's gleaming trophies. A marble staircase leads to a warren of rooms that have balconies with sweeping views of the village.

Premlata Singh is sitting on a charpoy in the concrete courtyard, wearing a salwar kameez with a gold ring in her nose and slippers on her feet. Other than the sharp eyes that gleam out of her doughy face there is virtually no resemblance between her and her fierce young daughter. Singh isn't a wrestler, she isn't educated, and when Phogat was born she wasn't even pleased to meet her.

Singh was brought up believing that girls simply cost their family a dowry before dedicating their energies to their husband. One of her two sons died when he was a few days old. She prayed for another but ended up with two daughters, the second of whom was Phogat. 'I thought,

Right: A wrestler at the Sir Chhotu Ram Stadium under a photo of Olympic champion Sakshi Malik, winner of a bronze medal at the Rio de Janeiro Games of 2016 and an ex-pupil of the school.

"Two girls, oh no, what an expense!" I didn't know any better. No one did.' Even as a child Phogat understood her lowly place in the hierarchy. '*Galti hoon main, galti!*' she would shout in frustration. 'I am a mistake, a mistake!'

The state of Haryana is unusually conservative, even by the standards of rural India. India as a whole has a skewed gender ratio because boys are so prized that many female foetuses are aborted. But in Haryana the ratio is especially uneven: 831 girls are born for every 1,000 boys, compared with the national rate of 940 to 1,000. Girls are often fed less than boys. 'If the buffalo gives one glass of milk,' it is said there, 'give it to the boy. The girl will drink water.' What made Singh stand out was that, despite her own upbringing, she unlearned these ideas.

When Phogat was eight years old her father Rajpal, a bus driver, was shot dead by a relative after an argument. It was unheard of for Hindu widows to live alone, and many ended up marrying their brothers-in-law. Singh declined Rajpal's brother's suggestion of moving in with him. 'No thank you,' she said. 'I will look after my own children.' Premlata throws her head back and laughs as she remembers that time. And, just like that, she resembles her daughter Vinesh, celebrating gleefully after outwitting yet another opponent.

Singh's decision led to uproar. Family members from distant villages were summoned to convince her to change her mind.

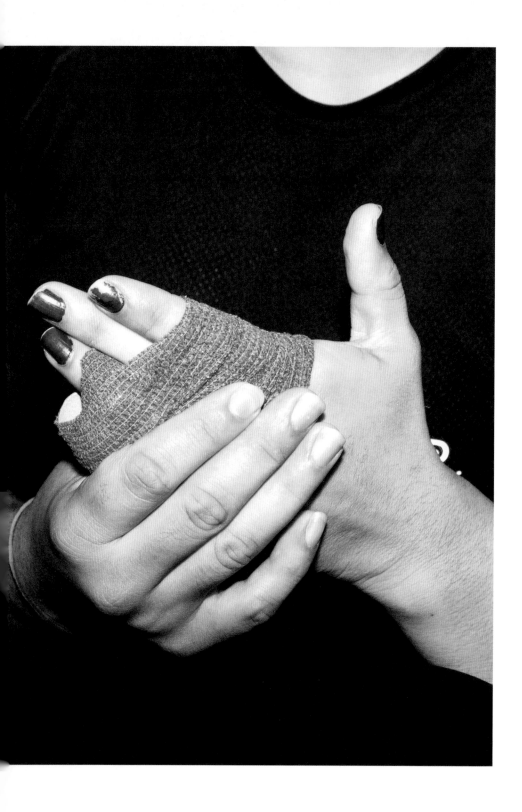

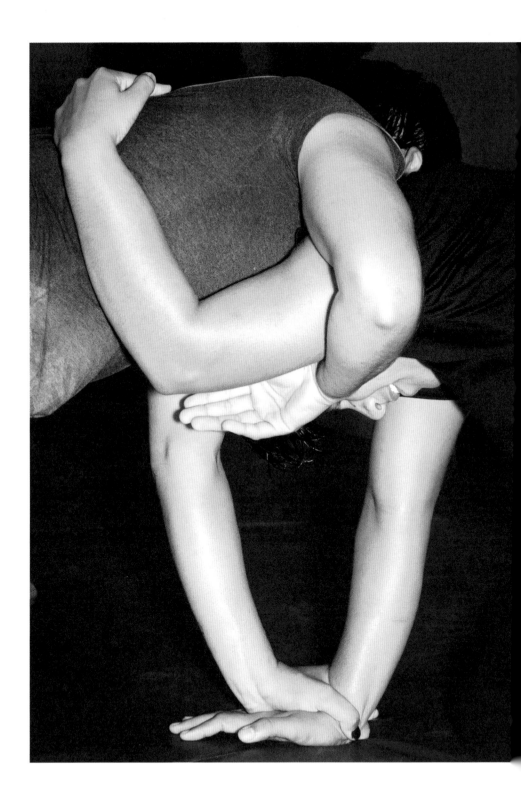

She had recently been diagnosed with uterine cancer, and there was no way that she would manage without help, she was told. But she survived the cancer – 'I outwitted the doctor,' she chortles – and she proved resilient and imaginative.

She fed her children milk, yogurt and clarified butter from the four buffaloes the family owned. With her husband's pension she started a micro-finance business, charging interest on loans to other women in the village. Singh wasn't familiar with traditional counting systems, so she invented her own. Her business venture, which was the first of its kind in the village run by a woman, was a success. 'I just told myself I can do it,' she said. '"I can do it! I can do it!" And then I did it.' Gradually, the objections to her single parenting quietened.

'My mother took a stand,' Phogat says. 'She was strong. And because of her I am strong, too.'

With the exception of cricketing victories, India has a terrible sporting record. It has the lowest number of Olympic medals per head of any nation and has only ever won one gold in an individual sport, the men's ten-metre air rifle. In recent years this has begun to change, partly owing to the changing role of women. At the Sydney Olympics in 2000 a weightlifter called Karnam Malleswari lifted 240 kilograms to win a bronze medal, the first Indian woman to make it that far in an Olympic sport. That she had overcome great obstacles amplified her achievement. Malleswari,

who lived in Haryana, had trained in a thatched shed with barbells made from bamboo and rocks. After her victory the state government gave her a plot of land and a cheque for $35,000.

Watching all this was Mahavir Singh, Phogat's uncle. What grabbed his attention was the government's prize for a gold medallist: ten million rupees, almost $140,000. Like Phogat's mother, Mahavir had often wondered what he would do with the four daughters the Hindu gods had given him. Now he knew. He would train them to win the biggest jackpot in Indian sporting history.

Wrestling was the obvious sport to try. Its traditional form, in which men fight in mud pits, was wildly popular in Haryana. Wrestling competitions, or dangals, attracted thousands of spectators who treated such events like a carnival. Mahavir – a hefty man with a broad nose, thick eyebrows and slanted eyes which give him a look of perpetual scepticism – had himself competed in these tournaments in the 1970s and 1980s, travelling along dusty highways in the back of bullock carts and sleeping outdoors to fight in villages. But, although he had won dozens of prizes, his father forced him to stop wrestling in his early twenties to get a 'real' job. Mahavir never forgave him – 'I would have fought in international tournaments.' He channelled his thwarted ambition and his desire for money into the next generation – his daughters and nieces.

Phogat remembers that she, her sister and her cousins were roused from bed at 4 a.m. on a freezing morning when she was only six years old. Winter had already settled on the mustard fields around Balali, but Mahavir marched the girls outside into the biting air. First they had to run laps of the fields to get their blood pumping. Then they were paired up to wrestle as best they could. Every day he made them practise for six hours. He beat them if they were late. He beat them for being slow to pick themselves up. He beat them for losing. Once he beat Phogat with such force that some of the villagers came running out to rescue her. The villagers nicknamed him 'Devil'.

'He wanted an Olympic medal,' Phogat says. 'We didn't even know what the Olympics were. "Who the hell is this Olympics?" we'd wonder. "We're being beaten black and blue, but Olympics still hasn't shown up!"'

When Mahavir got the man who trimmed the buffaloes to cut off the girls' long, silky hair, the villagers decided that he was crazy and best left alone. Who will marry his daughters now? they tutted.

To begin with the girls wrestled each other in a mud pit that Mahavir dug for them. They sometimes had to compete against boys in dangals. The first time Mahavir's eldest daughter, Geeta, participated, the bout was over after a few minutes. 'Geeta quickly grabbed the boy by the arm, pulled him over her shoulder and pinned him down,' says journalist Saurabh Duggal, who has written a biography of Mahavir. 'The mud stains on his back at the end of the bout reflected his quick defeat.'

Geeta was the most successful in the early years, but Phogat was also starting to distinguish herself. She was the smallest of the group but the first to arrive for practice. Already she was displaying certain attributes common to most elite athletes – an obsessive love of her chosen sport, intense focus and an overwhelming desire to win. 'I practised like a crazy person,' she says. 'Then I'd come home and train in my room.'

Local competitions led to regional and then national trials. At the Commonwealth Games in Delhi in 2010 Geeta won the country's first ever gold medal in wrestling.

WRESTLING

Wrestling, or *pehlwani*, is hugely popular across the whole of the Indian subcontinent. This has its roots in the 16th century, when the Muslim Mughal dynasty conquered northern India and blended the Persian practice of *koshti pahlavani* with the Indian *malla-yuddha* wrestling. The success of films such as *Dangal* ('Wrestling Competition') and *Sultan* ('King') and the multiple victories of north-Indian wrestler Vinesh Phogat have strengthened the perception that wrestling is primarily a phenomenon of the north based in the state of Haryana, but Maharashtra state and the city of Kolhapur (which has the country's largest arena with a capacity of thirty thousand people) also have a long tradition of *kushti*, a local form of wrestling. The first ever Olympic medal to be won by India in an individual competition (in Helsinki, 1952) was thanks to a wrestler from this area, Khashaba Dadasaheb Jadhav. The wrestlers almost always come from rural backgrounds, and in periods of extreme dry weather they often have to leave their taleems – academies in which they live and train as a community – to help their families. Indian athletes, accustomed to training on red sand and observing different rules, find it difficult to get used to wrestling on mats in international competitions. The sport also has iconic status in Pakistan, where people still venerate Ghulam Mohammad Baksh Butt, known as the 'Great Gama', who remained unbeaten throughout his career. Despite this, the number of akharas, training centres, is decreasing throughout the country. As far away as Dubai there are many *pehlwani* fans, often immigrants from India keen to keep up with their passion for the sport of their homeland, even at a distance.

THE COMMONWEALTH GAMES

The tradition of organising a sporting competition once every four years between the best athletes from the countries of the former British Empire dates to 1930 and has managed to survive the process of decolonisation. Initially known as the British Empire Games, the Commonwealth Games has now taken place twenty-one times: it includes fifty-three nations and five thousand athletes, confirming the competition as one of the biggest sporting events in the world, despite the fact that many of the Olympic giants – including China, the USA, Russia and the countries of continental Europe – do not compete. The programme for the games is chosen by the host nation, and in addition to core disciplines included in every games – such as swimming, athletics, field hockey, badminton, table tennis, bowls and squash – the hosts sometimes add other sports, although the number of team sports is limited to four. There is no separate event for para-athletes, who are, instead, included as full members of the national teams, making it the first inclusive, international multisport event. Although the Indian haul of Olympic medals is somewhat meagre, the country boasts a total of 504 Commonwealth medals, including 181 gold, making it the fourth most successful country after Australia, England and Canada. The Sports Federation of India threatened a boycott when it was announced that shooting would not be among the nineteen disciplines in the 2022 Games – after field hockey, shooting is India's most successful sport in terms of medals – but was persuaded against doing so by the central government.

Hundreds of villagers made the trip from Balali to cheer her on. When she returned, many more gathered at the entrance of the village to garland her with marigolds. Geeta and her sister Babita, who won a silver medal, received around $175,000 for their performance at the games from the state government. It wasn't long before Phogat also started winning. In 2013 she got a silver medal at the Youth Wrestling Championship in Johannesburg and then crowned this with a gold at the Commonwealth Games in Glasgow the following year.

Money flowed. Mahavir refurbished a room in the village for the girls to wrestle in. He bought mats and set up a fully equipped gym. He expanded his family's home into a fortress-like compound and drove a new car.

'Mahavir's fortunes changed because of his daughters,' says Rudraneil Sengupta, author of *Enter the Dangal: Travels Through India's Wrestling Landscape* (Harper Sport, 2016). With the influx of visible and previously unimaginable wealth, local villagers stopped protesting about how he trained the girls. Fathers now sought him out for advice on how to get their daughters into wrestling.

A couple of days after her victory in the 2019 Pro Wrestling League, Phogat was eating breakfast at a relative's house in Kharkhoda, a city in Haryana, where she and her husband had come for a family visit. Her physiotherapist joined her at the table, dressed in a nearly identical tracksuit. Hunched over their plates, the two scooped curd into their mouths. The stillness of the morning was broken only by sizzling sounds from the kitchen, where the cook was frying parathas. Phogat's husband Rathee, whom she married in 2018, pottered around in the background, gathering her kit for practice.

Rathee first saw Phogat when she was fifteen and eating an ice cream after a competition. He was eighteen at the time, and, like her, he had just started out on the national championship circuit. 'One day I'll marry that girl,' he told a friend. He was being serious, but it was hard to take him seriously: floppy-haired and serene, Rathee is so shy he has difficulty looking people in the face. Two years elapsed before he summoned the courage to call Phogat.

'Listen,' she cut him off. 'This is my mother's phone. Call again and she will thrash me. And she will thrash you, too.'

Their relationship mostly played out on their devices. They messaged each other on Facebook. They texted. And even as they shared photographs as keepsakes they told no one. In their rural community, Rathee says, 'girls don't talk to boys. If they do people don't respect them.' The young couple were afraid that if their relationship became known among the state's small wrestling community the gossip and derision that would inevitably follow would hurt Phogat's career. Rathee, who is also from Haryana, was determined to keep her on track. 'My mother had to ask my father for permission to leave the house,' he says. 'What were her interests? No one asked. What were her dreams? No one knew. We didn't even know what was on her mind ... I didn't want that. I thought, "I'm going to let my wife do whatever she wants."'

Phogat burst out laughing at the idea of waiting around for a man to give her the OK. 'I don't listen to anyone,' she said, 'not even to you.'

When she was younger she did whatever her Uncle Mahavir said. He prescribed the diet that traditional wrestlers followed, avoiding meat to appease the Hindu gods. She relied on talismans rather than modern medicine to heal her injuries. Despite her early success neither her stamina nor her technique was sufficient. After her victory in Glasgow it took her four years to win another championship gold.

In 2016 Aamir Khan, one of India's biggest Bollywood stars, released a film based on her family. Khan, a small, lean man, packed on twenty-five kilograms to play Mahavir. Called *Dangal*, the film shows how Mahavir trained his children to become wrestlers, despite opposition from the other villagers. The film had all the elements of a great Bollywood story – drama, action, a rousing score. It had the added benefit of being true to the facts. In the end, the actress who plays Geeta wins a gold medal in the Commonwealth Games. *Dangal* quickly became the highest-grossing Indian film ever made, netting over $300 million worldwide. Suddenly the Phogats started appearing on magazine covers and television talk shows.

For some members of the family this was the apogee of their careers. But it was a low time for Phogat. She had qualified for the Rio Olympics that summer and was tipped to win a medal, but in the quarter-finals she snapped her knee and had to be carried out on a stretcher. '*Gayaa, sab gayaa*,' she wept. 'Gone, all gone.' It didn't help that the film everyone kept asking her about didn't even mention her. *Dangal* focused exclusively on Mahavir's two eldest daughters. Phogat had long known that her uncle favoured his own children: on one occasion he refused to let Phogat attend a trial she had qualified for, insisting that one of his daughters take her place. Although he had no say in the film,

for her this was further evidence of his preference.

Phogat used her enforced rest after Rio to break with the old ways – Mahavir and his methods were the first to go.

'She started from zero,' says Vinay Siwach, a sports journalist. For the first time she acquired a professional coach, Wöller Ákos, a Hungarian wrestler who now works with her full time. Her physiotherapist also travels with her. She added a nutritionist, a psychologist and a sparring partner. All of this was funded by Olympic Gold Quest, a non-profit organisation aimed at helping Indian athletes win Olympic medals. In the run-up to the next Olympics in Tokyo, the foundation will spend around $400,000 to give Phogat the support that she needs to beat the Japanese, who are the best freestyle wrestlers in the world. It is all far removed from the mud pits, beatings and folk medicine of her uncle's training days.

'Now I surround myself with people who believe in my dream,' she says. 'Tokyo will be mine.'

For Phogat, victory means far more than a medal. 'There's a wrestler in every family in Haryana,' she says, 'but they have always been men. Now women see a clear path forward. "She looks just like me," they say.' Every win she has makes it easier for other women to see themselves as fighters.

At least twenty-five schools in India now train women to be freestyle wrestlers. Haryana and other states organise more competitions in rural areas and offer the

most accomplished competitors free training and monthly stipends. Medal-winning athletes are rewarded with secure government jobs on the railways, in the army or the police – even Phogat has a managerial job with the Indian state railway, as does her husband. Her role comes with perks and a pension, but as long as she is wrestling she will never have to show up for work. The government hopes that such programmes will encourage more women to wrestle and become champions. One day, perhaps, wrestling in India will be a sport identified with women as much as with men.

After Phogat had finished her breakfast of curd and parathas that morning, she slipped into her singlet, grabbed her mat shoes and headed to a local gym housed on the top floor of a three-storey building in a private school for boys. The setting wasn't what she was used to: the weight machines were old and rusty, and monkeys clung to the bars on the windows as parrots flew by outside. Her companions at the gym that morning were a few dozen teenagers in bright tracksuits hoping to represent India on the wrestling mat.

Phogat slipped on her hot-pink shoes and straightened her pony-tail. Wearing a flinty expression, her jaw jutting, she did some light stretches and jogged around the hall to loosen up. Then she noticed her husband looking distracted. Without a moment's hesitation she lunged for his ankle, heaved him up and flipped him over her shoulder. From the ground he gave his wife a huge grin and threw himself at her. Rathee said jokingly that he likes to let his wife win.

Phogat snorted at the idea. 'Let's go again,' she said, half seriously. 'I don't let anyone win.' 🖋

There's No Such Thing as Indian Literature

Nine administrative units, twenty-eight states, over 120 languages spoken (twenty-two of them official), each with their own dialects: the idea of Indian literature as a single entity is a fallacy. Arunava Sinha selects four books that represent four different literary traditions in this short guide to the countless voices of modern India.

ARUNAVA SINHA

Left: A barber reads a newspaper on a Varanasi ghat.

There is no one literature of India; there are, however, many literatures of India, each of them born out of a different language, living and breathing in the unique cultural web that a language represents. Often these different literatures have little in common, for, in a different paradigm of geography, the states of India – most of which have their own language – would actually have been separate countries.

The linguistic diversity of India is unparalleled when compared with any other country in the world. The eyes as well as the mind glaze over at the numbers: between them the people who live within the political boundaries of India speak nearly twenty thousand different tongues – granted, these can be clustered into similar languages, but, even so, more than 120 distinct languages, each with their attendant dialects, can be identified. Of course, the official (read: for the purposes of administration) number of languages in India is twenty-two. With twenty-eight separate states and nine other administrative units, the union territories, it is easy to see that each of the official languages can be traced back to one or more of these states. Indeed, a number of states were formed explicitly along linguistic lines to enable their residents to develop a language-based identity – which, of course, is only one of the many identities to which an 'Indian' can lay claim.

All of these twenty-two languages have their own distinct literatures, as do many of the other tongues that do not have that official status. In fact, if the idea of literature were not to be confined to printed books alone it wouldn't be an exaggeration to say that India has thousands of individual literatures. And the country has always worn this plurality comfortably, even though the language called Hindi has grown to become the one used – including all its variations – by almost half the country, the northern half to be precise.

As a result, the idea of a single Indian literature is an imaginary one, a box crafted by the publishing business for world markets by editors and curators seeking order and structure in the gloriously chaotic multiplicity of literatures from India and, increasingly, by the cultural project of the right-wing Hindu-nationalist organisation, the Rashtriya Swayamsevak Sangh (RSS) – the ideological backbone of the BJP, which is currently in power in the country – to impose cultural homogeneity as a tool of control over a population that thrives on diversity and cannot be managed conveniently. The preferred language of much of the publishing industry in India is English, for the simple reason that it is globally accepted and acts as a standard for the world's publishers. As for the RSS, its preferred language is Hindi, for not only is it the most used language it is also rooted in the BJP heartlands.

ARUNAVA SINHA is a translator and associate professor of practice in creative writing at Ashoka University, Haryana, who translates classical, modern and contemporary literature from Bengali into English. He has twice won the Crossword Book Award, in 2007 for the translation of *Chowringhee* by Sankar and in 2011 for *17* by Anita Agnihotri. His translations, around sixty to date, have been published in the USA, UK and India.

INDIAN LANGUAGES

How many are there? Some people say 780, others talk of two thousand dialects, and then there's the constitution, which recognises twenty-two (with thirty-eight waiting to be awarded official status). The most spoken language is Hindi, with 528 million speakers, followed by Bengali with ninety-seven million, Marathi with eighty-three million, Telugu with eighty-one million, Tamil with sixty-nine million and Gujarati with fifty-five million. How many newspapers would you find on a well-stocked Indian stand? There are, for example, thirty-six daily newspapers in Punjabi, twenty-five in Marathi, twenty-three in Kannada, sixteen in Malayalam and eighteen in Tamil. The newspaper with the highest circulation in the country, *Dainik Jagran*, is in Hindi (as are those with the second- and third-highest circulations),

and strangely it has sixteen million readers whereas 'only' 2.6 million copies are printed: each copy is shared around eight people. The range of newspapers in regional languages is increasing, especially in outlying areas where literacy levels are rising. The publishing industry, however, is dominated by English, which accounts for 55 per cent of all publications. This sector is growing, too, with 1,500 novels published each year, and it is now the sixth-largest world market. Of all non-English publications, 35 per cent are in Hindi. Most texts in other languages are translated from English and then, using that version, into Hindi, so there is a high risk of loss of authenticity. Despite the fact that, according to the constitution, the use of English for official purposes should have stopped in 1965, it maintains its status as an intermediary language as well as a language of emancipation, mobility and opportunity.

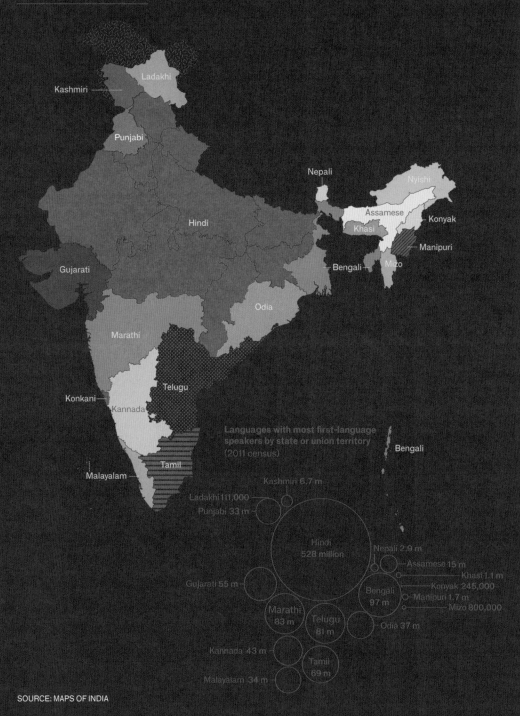

Kashmiri

Ladakhi

Punjabi

Nepali

Nyishi

Assamese

Konyak

Khasi

Hindi

Manipuri

Gujarati

Mizo

Bengali

Odia

Marathi

Konkani

Telugu

Kannada

Languages with most first-language
speakers by state or union territory
(2011 census)

Bengali

Malayalam

Tamil

Kashmiri 6.7 m

Ladakhi 111,000

Punjabi 33 m

Hindi
528 million

Nepali 2.9 m

Assamese 15 m

Khasi 1.1 m

Gujarati 55 m

Konyak 245,000

Bengali
97 m

Manipuri 1.7 m

Marathi
83 m

Mizo 800,000

Telugu
81 m

Odia 37 m

Kannada 43 m

Tamil
69 m

Malayalam 34 m

SOURCE: MAPS OF INDIA

*

Thanks to this attempt at cultural monolingualism, Hindi is getting a reputation it does not deserve, because, far from being a political tool, it is, in fact, one of the more than a dozen languages whose literatures are now beginning to find their place in the stream of books that are read all over the country and not just in their own region. Paradoxically, this has been enabled by a robust practice of translating works from the non-English languages into English – a language that is genuinely pan-Indian – and the publication of these works by the largest Indian-language publishers.

In the process, these translations are not only edging inwards from the periphery to share the central space with books originally written in English – increasingly, readers are picking their English-language titles without discriminating between translations and original works in English – but they are also bringing to the old Anglophone tradition new ways of writing and reading in English. Often dealing with themes from the ordinary, everyday lives of underprivileged, even oppressed, people, these novels from other languages probably could not have been written in English, a language in which the writer's vantage point in India has tended to be cerebral and distant rather than earthy and even raw.

One acknowledgement of this enrichment of the literary space is that at least five major literary awards in the region for English-language books – the JCB Prize for Literature, the DSC Prize for South Asian Literature, the Hindu Prizes for fiction and for non-fiction and the New India Foundation Prize for non-fiction – consider books originally written in English and translated into English on an equal footing, even offering some of the prize money to the translators. It does not require a particularly keen eye to see that the literary landscape is changing.

As points on the map of this emerging territory, we look at four novels in four different languages from India – Malayalam, the language of the state of Kerala; Hindi, the language of most parts of northern and central India; Kannada, the language of the state of Karnataka; and Bengali, the language of the state of West Bengal as well as of the country of Bangladesh.

MALAYALAM

Aarachar (2012)
K.R. Meera
Translated into English by J. Devika
Hangwoman (Penguin, 2016)

Even in the 21st century, women across India constantly have to prove themselves capable of doing the work that men have claimed as their preserve. Controlled by males, most segments of the economy make room for women only grudgingly. It is partly against this backdrop that the Malayalam writer K.R. Meera places her novel *Aarachar*, translated into English as *Hangwoman* by J. Devika. Meera, however, chooses not a modern, corporate backdrop but a rather unlikely one – the business of hanging prisoners who have been sentenced to death.

In Meera's novel, set – unexpectedly perhaps for a writer from Kerala – in Bengal, 22-year-old Chetna Grddha Mullick is thrown into a situation she might not have anticipated. Her father, Phanibhushan

Page 179: A street vendor reads the paper in Old Delhi, a neighbourhood of India's capital.

Grddha Mullick, the last male in a family with a lineage going back thousands of years, whose traditional occupation is hanging condemned criminals, is now too old to do the job – and there is a new prisoner waiting to be hanged. Choosing not to disrupt the family line, Chetna decides she will take over. Or does she really? Is it possible that she has been manipulated by a sensationalist media?

This imaginative exploration of the position of women in contemporary India eliminates the possibility of pussyfooting around the subject by placing Chetna Grddha Mullick in a stark, raw situation that stands at the intersection of a number of social and political forces. There is no opportunity here for a sophisticated, academic analysis – this is an urgent, vibrant, rich and relentless novel that deftly constructs the messily complex theatre in which the drama – and it is nothing less than drama – plays out.

The very issue of capital punishment and whether it is reserved only for the oppressed, plays as a constant counterpoint to Mullick's journey. But make no mistake, this is not fiction masquerading as polemic; even if it is not plot driven, *Hangwoman* is replete with fleshed-out characters and an uncanny sense of place. Most interestingly, it inserts itself into the literary stream not just of Kerala but also of Bengal, in a sense forming a bridge between two cultures where lives are not lived in English, deploying one as a viewing platform and the other as the location. Unlikely as it may seem given its subject matter, Meera's novel is more successful at framing, probing and navigating the space of feminism in India than other contemporary works that take on the same issues with a more direct approach. It is a triumph of fiction in telling some of the truths on the Indian subcontinent today.

KANNADA

Ghachar Ghochar (2013)
Vivek Shanbhag

Translated into English by Srinath Perur
Ghachar Ghochar (Penguin, 2017 USA /
Faber & Faber, 2018 UK)

The big-bang economic liberalisation of India in 1991 was like a switch suddenly being thrown that opened up the middle class to the prospect of a sudden improvement in income, material wealth and property ownership. Thousands of families in dozens of cities across the country found themselves climbing out of stagnant earnings and low-intensity consumption to join the ranks of carefree consumers. Something, however, got left behind in the mad rush to acquire homes, cars, gadgets and lifestyles: honesty and ethics.

Vivek Shanbhag's novel *Ghachar Ghochar*, written in Kannada, is the story of a Bangalore family caught in this transition from a life of strained means to one of sudden affluence. Shanbhag skilfully creates a moral knot in the lives of the members of this family as they struggle to deal with their new-found prosperity, which threaten the values with which they had lived previously.

A seemingly small novel, *Ghachar Ghochar* is, in fact, a vast telling of an entire society through the trajectory of one family. With an unreliable and somewhat vacuous narrator relating the story, primarily in the form of a play of personal insecurities, the apparent focus is on whether or not an act of extreme violence has taken place. But perhaps more important is the way Shanbhag builds the milieu with loving attention to minutiae seemingly unrelated to the main story – such as the floorplan of the house the family used to live in, regular attacks by ants – but actually feeding it with details that enable the reader to envision the middle-class existence of a family in the state of Karnataka with every member deeply invested in one another's personal progress, until the effects of a sudden influx of money kick in.

The title of the novel signifies an impossibly snarled drawstring, a phrase coined by one of the characters, which effortlessly represents the state of affairs for the main characters. And in the figure of Vincent – the waiter at the coffee house to whom the narrator makes many of his confessions but who always seems to know more than he lets on – *Ghachar Ghochar* offers a fascinating version of the reader/listener, the 'all-knowing public' that represents collective wisdom in India. This slim novel leaves you with the aftertaste of having read a monumental work of fiction.

BENGALI

Hajar Churashir Ma (1974)
Mahasweta Devi
Translated into English by Samik Bandyopadhyay
Mother of 1084 (Seagull Books, 2014)

The violent uprising that an extremist faction that grew out of the communist parties of India tried to bring about in the 1960s and 1970s – vestiges of which remain in some rural pockets – provides the setting for activist and writer Mahasweta Devi's clear-eyed 1974 novel. The movement was played out through attempts to overturn the existing structure of political power with guns and bombs, mostly homemade, by groups of young women and men who drew their inspiration from not just Marx but also Lenin – hence the name Communist Party of India (Marxist–Leninist) – and who operated mostly in the state of West Bengal, especially in its capital, Kolkata.

It is his participation in this armed uprising that leads to the killing of Brati, whose identity is reduced to that of corpse number 1084 in the morgue; his mother, Sujata, through whose grief and pride, love and resilience, this novel unfolds, is the mother of the title. Through Sujata's conflicts Mahasweta Devi merges both the external political turmoil – pitting class against class, society against the establishment, firebrands against the authorities – and the internal, familial one of the mother/wife/daughter figure who is seeking freedom and equality on her own behalf as well as womankind in general. Sujata never stops being the mother of the slain Brati, with the novel taking readers through the anguish that stays with her years after his killing as well as her memories of his transformation into an urban revolutionary.

Sujata is not welcome within her own family, whose members blame her for indulging Brati, and she is weighed down by the guilt of having allowed a distance to grow between herself and her son. And so this novel offers an unsentimental journey through the mind and heart of a mother whose depth of feeling is unclouded by cheap emotion – she doesn't even weep on hearing of her son's death. What *Mother of 1084* does is to dwell on the impact of the violent political movement of the Naxalites, as they were called, on the middle-class lives of the families whose daughters and sons chose to join this quest for change instead of passively accepting the continuing injustices suffered by the oppressed classes.

Things may have changed in the fifty years since the Naxalite movement was founded, but the injustices remain and with it the anaesthetising of the urban family who turn a blind eye to such injustices. And this is why *Mother of 1084* remains relevant today.

HINDI

The Walls of Delhi: Three Stories (2014)
Uday Prakash
Translated into English by Jason Grunebaum
The Walls of Delhi: Three Stories (Seven Stories Press, 2014)

Delhi is not only the capital city of India but it is, arguably, the space that best represents the bewildering confusion of a country at cross-purposes with its past and future, where thousands of different groups try every moment to negotiate survival, well-being, success, identity, relationships and, most of all, shortcuts to wealth. Naturally, one individual's accomplishment is often another's ruination in this constant collision between people and their ambitions. Reality often turns absurdist as rules break down, systems collapse and madcap innovation triumphs.

The Walls of Delhi, a collection of three stories by Uday Prakash, captures this gestalt with consummate skill, presenting scenarios that would be completely unreal if they weren't so plausible in the maelstrom that is modern urban India. As Delhi – standing in for India as a whole – is constantly rebuilt, with older structures demolished to make way for new ones,

Right: Reading the paper on a street in Varanasi.

with the poor inevitably being elbowed out by the rich, hidden things emerge, making for stories that would not have been possible in any other space.

So in one story a sweeper finds a stash of money hidden away by someone trying to evade paying taxes, using it to take his distinctly underage lover to Agra for a glimpse of the fabled Taj Mahal, only to discover that being rich, even temporarily, comes with its own troubles. In the second story, a Dalit – a member of the oppressed castes in India's repulsive but extant caste system of discrimination on the basis of a person's lineage – finds his identity stolen by an upper-caste man who is trying to cash in on the benefits of affirmative action. And in the third, a family tries to cure a baby of its 'illness' of extreme intelligence, represented by an ever-growing head.

As Uday Prakash emphasises through his far-from-linear narratives, in each of these stories life does not proceed from point A to point B in orderly, predictable ways in the constantly changing landscape of contemporary India. The chaos of the external world combines with the lack of stability in personal lives to turn what could have been a tranquil pursuit of a better existence into a raging storm that uproots all certainties. Art and life blend into one.

*

In each of these four books – as, indeed, every book translated from one of the Indian languages into English – the work of the translators is absolutely invaluable. It is only thanks to their mission that literature in the English language is so wondrously diverse today, and that the literature of Indian writers in English is no longer the only one to present the many Indias to the global reader. ✦

A Sign of
the Times

GIOIA GUERZONI
Translated by Jennifer Higgins

For lovers of vintage *kaali-peeli* taxis, 2020 was a terrible year. Production of the iconic black-and-yellow vehicles stopped in 2000 and – following the 2013 legislation by the Mumbai authorities whereby all taxis are to be decommissioned after twenty years – the few dozen still running at the start of 2020 would have to be taken out of service during the course of the year. Also known as Padminis, these cars are only found in the 'Big Mango' and not in Delhi or Kolkata, where the iconic Hindustan Ambassador reigned supreme until 2011, when new emissions laws meant they, too, stopped being built.

The Mumbai black-and-yellow made its debut in 1964 as the Fiat 1100 Delight, and in 1974 was reborn as the Premier Padmini, named after the legendary medieval queen. Although not as spacious as the Ambassador, they were tough and easy to maintain and became so popular that by the 1990s there were more than 63,000 of them in the city. In 2013, in the Mumbai metropolitan region there were around a hundred thousand licences for the black-and-yellows, far more taxi licences than in any other city in the world: in Beijing, there are about sixty thousand and fifty thousand in New York. It's difficult to calculate the number of taxis per head, because there is a greater concentration in the south of the city. South Mumbai sits on a long, narrow strip of land; it is comparable to Manhattan in this and also in its astronomical property prices and consequent social make-up. Here the otherwise ubiquitous three-wheeled auto rickshaws are banned. While the northern areas of the city buzz with the sound of Piaggio Apes and other varieties – which are cheaper than a car over short distances – in the south there is approximately one taxi for every sixty inhabitants, a very high number when compared with, say, Milan, which has one taxi per three hundred inhabitants, or Paris, which has one for every two hundred.

Riding in a Padmini can be an almost psychedelic experience. As well as the

nimbu-mirchi, strings of limes and chillies, hanging from the rear-view mirror to ward off evil spirits and bad luck. Rather like the *cornetto* good-luck charms traditionally used in Naples, *nimbu-mirchi* can also be made from plastic. Photographs of favourite actors are also common: from Amitabh Bachchan to Shah Rukh Khan, from Aishwarya Rai to Katrina Kaif. And stickers, lots of stickers. The best is 'Please horn', an invitation to use a vehicle's horn in the interests of avoiding collisions with other road-users – including animals.

The most popular decorative elements, though, are the deities of Hinduism and other religions, from gurus to the Buddha via Jesus and Mary, the infant Krishna, Guru Nanak and so on. Here the drivers really go for it: mini altars with flashing lights, topped with a diminutive Ganesh or Lakshmi, statues of every shape and size fixed to the dashboard, plastic reproductions hanging from the rear-view mirror, fluorescent stickers in the corners of the windscreen, often big enough to obscure the driver's view. A joyful explosion of tacky, multi-faith goodwill. Muslim drivers usually have plainer vehicles because of restrictions on the images they can display: a page from the Qur'an or, more rarely, a *nazar* (evil eye) or hand of Fatima (*hamsa*) amulet. Little sacred books, usually in black and gold, hang from the mirror or are displayed on the dashboard.

Mumbai taxi drivers are true knights of the road: they survive in a harsh, expensive city, find ingenious ways of making ends meet, endure traffic jams, smog and pollution with stoicism, constantly face confrontation and, despite all this, will crack a smile and love a chat. After all, Mumbai is perhaps the only city in the world where, when the traffic lights are red, a word appears in the illuminated red circle: 'Relax'.

most common accessories – mini-fans on the dashboard, radios belting out songs in Hindi, coloured armrests, little mats to hang over the open windows to stop the sun-heated metal burning your arm – you occasionally find real gems: a chandelier swinging close to the driver's head, a ceiling covered in mirrors like a disco ball or even a vertical bar sticking up between the two rear seats. When you ask the driver what it's for, the answer, delivered in the gravest of tones, will be, 'It's like in the disco, pole dance.'

Then there are the seat coverings: beyond the classic black plastic there are other variants in pure synthetic materials, with diamonds, flowers, zebra stripes, 1970s wallpaper motifs ... Some drivers, wanting to protect the upholstery, cover them in polythene – not the most comfortable surface to sit on in humid Mumbai.

The knick-knacks and adornments deserve some notice, too. There are often clusters of fruit – usually plastic grapes – and many taxis have little bunches of

The Playlist

MATTEO MIAVALDI
Translated by Jennifer Higgins

You can listen to this playlist at:
open.spotify.com/user/iperborea

T ake two masters of Indian classical music, Krishna Bhatt and Zakir Hussain, put them together in a room in San Francisco in the 1980s, surround them with ageing hippies and make them play the raga *Jansammohini*: the result will be a half-hour snapshot of what people think of when they talk about 'Indian music'.

There is a whole world of Indian music beyond Ravi Shankar, the sitar legend who is – unfortunately – best known outside India for having taught George Harrison to play two or three licks. It's a world of fusion and exchange in the best Indian tradition: take something, make it your own and give it back enriched. So we have Hussain, the greatest living tabla player, flirting with jazz in his trio with Dave Holland and Chris Potter. Indian Ocean, the fathers of Indian fusion, mingle rock, classical and jazz, and Ananda Shankar, nephew of Ravi, collaborated with DJ State of Bengal shortly before his death, a partnership that was a milestone in electronica.

There is, however, an insatiable monster threatening the creative freedom of Indian artists: Bollywood. The world's most prolific cinema industry draws young talent into a constant treadmill of production, shutting them in inane, sugar-coated cages that make India's bigscreen fortune. It is likely that this will be the fate that will befall two of the country's most promising singer-songwriters, Prateek Kuhad and Lifafa. They are a far cry from the brothers Kalyanji and Anandji or from R.D. Burman, who were responsible for some of the best Indian psychedelic funk produced during the 1970s and 1980s, with the mellow voices of Asha Bhosle and Hemlata (represented in this playlist by a soft-porn track that would be inconceivable by today's puritanical Bollywood standards).

But while the country regresses in the face of rampant Hindu extremism, protest music is going through a golden age. From the quasi-Saharan funk-blues of Gauley Bhai from Bangalore to Divine and Naezy producing rap from the Mumbai slums.

Finally, two hot new projects full of fire and passion from Tamil Nadu: the Casteless Collective, who make folk rock against caste discrimination, and Arivu, whose hip-hop borrows from the hypnotic rhythms of the Tamil language.

1

Krishna
Bhatt & Zakir
Hussain
Jansammohini
1984

2

Dave Holland,
Zakir Hussain,
Chris Potter
Ziandi
2019

3

Indian Ocean
Bandeh
2005

4

Hemlata
*Na Na Na Yeh
Kya Karne
Lage Ho*
1980

5

Asha Bhosle
*Main Hoon
Lilly*
1984

6

The Ananda
Shankar
Experience
Betelnutters
1999

7

Lifafa
Jaago
2019

8

Divine & Naezy
Mere Gully Mein
2019

9

Gauley Bhai
Thupari Udi
2019

10

The Casteless
Collective
Quota
2018

11

Prateek Kuhad
Tune Kaha
2016

12

Arivu & ofRO
Kalla Mouni
2019

Further Reading

FICTION

Aravind Adiga
The White Tiger
Free Press, 2008 (USA) / Atlantic, 2012
(UK) / HarperCollins, 2009 (India)

Vikram Chandra
Sacred Games
Harper Perennial, 2007 (USA) / Faber &
Faber, 2007 (UK) / Penguin, 2008 (India)

Anita Desai
In Custody
Vintage, 2001 (UK) / Random
House, 2012 (India)

Kiran Desai
The Inheritance of Loss
Penguin, 2009 (USA) / Penguin,
2008 (UK) / Penguin, 2014 (India)

Mahasweta Devi
Breast Stories
Seagull Books, 2014

Amitav Ghosh
The Hungry Tide
Mariner Books, 2006 (USA) / HarperCollins,
2005 (UK) / HarperCollins, 2016 (India)

Manu Joseph
Serious Men
W.W. Norton, 2010 (USA) / John Murray,
2010 (UK) / HarperCollins, 2011 (India)

Jhumpa Lahiri
Interpreter of Maladies
Mariner Books, 2019 (USA) / Fourth Estate,
2019 (UK) / HarperCollins, 2005 (India)

Anita Nair
Ladies Coupé
Vintage, 2003 (USA, UK) /
Penguin, 2015 (India)

Salman Rushdie
Midnight's Children
Random House, 2006 (USA) /
Vintage, 2008 (UK)

Vikram Seth
A Suitable Boy
Harper Perennial, 2005 (USA) / Phoenix
House, 2013 (UK) / Aleph, 2014 (India)

Vikas Swarup
Q&A: A Novel
Scribner, 2008 (USA) / Black
Swan, 2006 (UK)

Jeet Thayil
Narcopolis
Penguin 2012 (USA) / Faber
& Faber, 2013 (UK)

Altaf Tyrewala
*Engglishhh: Fictional Dispatches
from a Hyperreal Nation*
Fourth Estate, 2014

NON-FICTION

Katherine Boo
*Behind the Beautiful Forevers: Life, Death,
and Hope in a Mumbai Undercity*
Random House, 2014 (USA) / Portobello,
2013 (UK) / Penguin, 2013 (India)

William Dalrymple
Nine Lives
Vintage, 2011 (USA) / Bloomsbury, 2016 (UK)

Rana Dasgupta
Capital: The Eruption of Delhi
Penguin, 2015 (USA) / Canongate, 2015 (UK)

Siddharta Deb
The Beautiful and the Damned: A Portrait of the New India (USA) / *The Beautiful and the Damned: Life in the New India* (UK, India)
Farrar, Straus and Giroux, 2012 (USA) / Penguin, 2012 (UK, India)

Dilip Hiro
The Longest August: The Unflinching Rivalry Between India and Pakistan
Nation Books, 2015

Prem Shankar Jha
Crouching Dragon, Hidden Tiger: Can China and India Dominate the West?
Soft Skull Press, 2009

Hermann Kulke and Dietmar Rothermund
A History of India
Routledge, 2016

Suketu Mehta
Maximum City: Bombay Lost and Found
Vintage, 2005 (USA) / Headline, 2005 (UK) / Penguin, 2017 (India)

Pankaj Mishra
Temptations of the West: How to Be Modern in India, Pakistan, Tibet, and Beyond
Picador, 2007 (USA, UK) / Penguin, 2013 (India)

V.S. Naipaul
India: A Wounded Civilization
Picador, 2010

Gavin D. Flood
An Introduction to Hinduism
CUP, 1996 (USA, UK)

Samanth Subramanian
Following Fish: Travels Around the Indian Coast
Atlantic, 2014 (USA) / Atlantic, 2013 (UK) / Penguin, 2011 (India)

Arundhati Roy
My Seditious Heart: Collected Non-fiction
Haymarket, 2019 (USA) / Hamish Hamilton, 2019 (UK, India)

Amartya K. Sen
The Argumentative Indian: Writings on Indian History, Culture and Identity
Picador, 2006

Vinay Sitapali
Jugalbandi: The BJP Before Modi
Viking, 2020 (India)

Annie Zaidi
Known Turf: Bantering with Bandits and Other True Tales
Westland, 2010

Graphic design and art direction: Tomo Tomo and Pietro Buffa

Photography: Gaia Squarci
Photographic content curated by Prospekt Photographers

Illustrations: Edoardo Massa

Infographics and cartography: Pietro Buffa

Editorial consultant *The Passenger India*: Gioia Guerzoni

Managing editor (English-language edition): Simon Smith

Thanks to: Martina Barlassina, Irina Bordogna, Jacopo Crimi, Adriana Costanzo, Vrinda Dar, Antonio Della Valle, Pilar Maria Guerrieri, Suhasini Haidar, Manu Joseph, A.G. Krishna Menon, Francesco Merlini, Anna Nadotti, Stephanie Nolen, Daniela Pagani, Carlo Pizzati, Chiki Sarkar, Bina Sarkar Ellias, Samanth Subramanian, Lisette Verhagen

The opinions expressed in this publication are those of the authors and do not purport to reflect the views and opinions of the publishers.

http://europaeditions.com/thepassenger
http://europaeditions.co.uk/thepassenger
#ThePassengerMag

The Passenger – India
© Iperborea S.r.l., Milan, and Europa Editions, 2021

Translators: Italian – Daniel Armenti (editorial, infographics, timeline, sidebars), Jennifer Higgins (A Sign of the Times, Playlist, sidebars), Alan Thawley (The National Sport, Stories of Another India, sidebars, photographer's biography, standfirsts); German – Jana Marlene Mader

All translations © Iperborea S.r.l., Milan, and Europa Editions, 2021, except 'Holding Back the Night' © Julia Lauter 2021

ISBN 9781787702967

Printed on Munken Pure thanks to the support of Arctic Paper

Printed by ELCOGRAF S.p.A., Verona, Italy